MARGIT TAKÁCS

Change Matters

Stories About Taming The Corporate Jungle and Leading Transformation

Copyright © 2023 by Margit Takács

All rights reserved. No part of this publication may be reproduced, stored, or transmitted in any form or by any means, electronic, mechanical, photocopying, recording, scanning, or otherwise, without the prior written permission of the publisher. Unauthorised reproduction, distribution, or transmission of this book, including posting it on a website or sharing it through any other means, is strictly prohibited by law.

The author, Margit Takács, asserts her moral right to be identified as the creator of this work. Margit Takács bears no responsibility for the persistence or accuracy of URLs for external or third-party internet websites mentioned in this publication and does not guarantee the continued accuracy or appropriateness of any content found on such websites.

Trademark designations used by companies to distinguish their products are often claimed as trademarks. All brand names and product names mentioned in this book, including those on its cover, are trade names, service marks, trademarks, or registered trademarks of their respective owners. The publishers and this book are not affiliated with any products or vendors mentioned herein. None of the companies referenced within the book have endorsed it.

First edition.

With thanks to:
Andrew Mark, author coach and collaborative writer
Dali de Clair, proofreader
German Valencia, mentor
Matías Thourte, illustrator
Maryna Beukes, book cover designer
Sole Bassett, graphic designer
Brenda van Rensburg, copy editor

To my incredible husband José Luis, and my precious daughters Evelyn and Ariana, thank you for your endless love and unwavering belief in me.

Life is beautiful with you.

Foreword

It is with great pride that I accepted the opportunity to write the foreword for this remarkable book, *Change Matters*. I have had the privilege of witnessing Margit's growth over the years as a change leader from a transformational program perspective as well as from our mentoring relationship. Throughout our journey, I have seen her dedication, passion, and unwavering commitment to bringing about positive change in the world and the result is what you hold in your hands now.

Change Matters reflects Margit's deep understanding of the significance of change and its transformative power. In this book, you have a collection of key messages that resonate with authenticity, insight, and a genuine desire to motivate and uplift readers. This book goes beyond the ordinary, diving deep into the essence of embracing change and navigating the unpredictable journey of life with resilience. I have first-hand experienced Margit's evolution as she embarked on this writing journey. Her deep-rooted belief in the potential for change shines through every word on these pages.

In 2015, Margit and her then-leader stepped into my office, offering to support me with the inevitable people resistance towards a global technology transformation program. I had already worked for decades on big change initiatives across the world. So, I knew too well that getting the technical solution ready and a capable squad behind to inspire others was key. My competent team was enthusiastic and ready for action, but I needed someone like Margit to join me to remind them of the human side of change and guide them to navigate the people landscape with success.

As we explored the program's burning platform, I knew that to get a change management consultant assigned to my initiative, I needed to speak the same language. Margit was observing as the dialogue progressed, assessed what could be leveraged, and at the end, she explained that she could 'only' guide the team in the journey with her expertise and methods, but we would need to be the face for the change. I wanted my team to be able to grow and learn to manage the human side better and better!

I remember when she first asked the key stakeholders to complete an initial change readiness assessment. We looked at the spiderweb chart showing the anonymous inputs and reflected on active and visible executive sponsorship and its strengths or weaknesses; the program management; the change management and communication elements of what we were about to embark on. I knew then that with Margit, we would go beyond theories as she would bring methods to constructive dialogues and practical work - exactly what I wanted - and we had the chance to work closely for a year.

After our transformation endeavour was successfully completed, she approached me again, but with a different intention: she asked me to be her mentor. I had already been mentoring several people as I believe in growing people, therefore the first thing I asked her was what she was committed to achieving and why I should mentor her. We had a lovely cup of tea in my office. The colourful autumn leaves of the trees by my office filtered in the sun as we talked about her aspirations.

I had seen her grow, both personally and professionally, and she let me share with her new perspectives when it came to managing one's energy for sustainable success and finding a true purpose. As we explored the most impactful phases of her life, we discovered her true calling in life as "catalysing change without borders," a calling that she continues to share with the world out there.

Fast forward to 2022; I received a pleasant message from Margit. She was no longer in the corporate world and had embarked on the path of being a business owner and independent change consultant. While she brings a great deal of expertise in the field, she asked if I could be her mentor again as she was ready to take her change management practice to a new level. Margit asked me to act as her guide, her cheerleader, and as a mirror, to allow her to see the world of entrepreneurs from a new perspective. I happily accepted her request to connect again.

It was during our second mentoring session in 2022 that she confidently shared about having started the writing of her book *Change Matters* on change management and leadership. I thought this was a brilliant idea to convey to the world what she stands for and what change she would like to bring about when it comes to a more human-centric realm. As I asked her about her 'why' for writing the book, she passionately explained her desire to share new insights into the challenges of human resistance. I immediately knew this was a calling worth pursuing.

Margit's guidance has undoubtedly shaped this book's profound insights and wisdom, making it a must-read with narrative storytelling for any change leader and practitioner seeking inspiration and a renewed perspective on the power of change.

As you embark on this enlightening and transformative journey through *Change Matters*, I encourage you to open your mind, embrace the stories, and reflect on the power you hold within yourself to make a difference and tackle the challenges described.

I am privileged to endorse *Change Matters* and its key messages. May this book serve as a beacon of hope, encouraging you to embrace change, step out of your comfort zone, and become the change you wish to see in the world. *Change Matters* is a great read, written by an author whose love of change, culture, and teashops I share!

With heartfelt gratitude,

German Valencia
Former Global C-suite Leader, Executive Advisor, Coach and Mentor

Contents

Introduction
13

Fight or Flight in the Quicksand
21

Trouble in Paradise
41

Fixing What isn't Broken
51

The Illusion of Alignment
69

The Bittersweet Journey of Bad News
83

Shower Hour and Killer Spiders
97

Million Dollar Decisions
115

The Pain in Spain
129

Part Two
143

Strength in Numbers
149

From Jungle to Safe Harbour
163

Acknowledgements
171

"Madártej"
181

Introduction

LEAP INTO NEW FRONTIERS

"Change is the law of life. And those who look only to the past or the present are certain to miss the future."
– John F. Kennedy

Writing this introduction has been difficult; ironically for the very reasons, I decided to write *Change Matters* in the first place. My first draft was penned right before the Covid pandemic. I listed a few current change events as examples and explained how this book, while about change, is also about my journey from intern to Global Director of Change Management in a large company that currently employs more than 590,000 staff and is active in 220 countries and territories.

Change is inevitable of course, and so, no sooner was the proverbial ink dry on my draft than another great change swept across the globe forcing me to rewrite this introduction. Pandemics, lockdowns, work from home, and now language model AI, chatbots, an awful war and a rapidly shifting geopolitical landscape are all added to my previous list of change examples. I should stop trying to list all the changes that are coming down the tracks for fear that I will never finish this introduction!

While this book is about change, and I hope it will be useful to change leaders and practitioners, it is not a university textbook. Instead, I use real stories from my career to illustrate key learning points from my journey. It is my wish that readers will find my experiences outlined in the narrative interesting and useful in their change journey.

I am an agent; a change agent. My most recent title was 'Global Engagement Director and Associate Director of Global Change Management' at a multi-national at the forefront of its industry. Over the years, my work has directly or indirectly impacted tens of thousands of lives and yet, very few of the people affected by my interventions even know my name.

Travelling the world helping teams and companies implement the changes necessary for their survival and global competitiveness, was both a privilege and an education. Working in some of the most difficult markets, across disparate cultures, allowed me to fill my strategy playbook in ways my university education never could.

My travels have taken me from the corporate world in the West to the jungles of Central America and as far away from there as the Asia Pacific region. Often, the only way for me to achieve the results expected by my organisation was to immerse myself completely in the local culture. Learning local habits, languages, and cultural norms was essential to my work.

It was in Asia that I cultivated an appreciation for the calming properties of tea. I also learnt that tea was a useful tool to use when I needed to pause a negotiation to gather my thoughts or to forge a bond with a new client.

Looking further back, my father was the main reason behind my embarking on this career. Both, my mom and my dad are teachers. And while my dad filled my head with knowledge, it was my mom who filled my heart with courage, resilience, and a belief in myself.

I grew up in Hungary in the tiny town of Békés. I have two brothers Ernő and András, presently, successful engineers, business leaders, and committed family men. They were also my triumphant minders during my childhood, ensuring I never came too close to the local boys. It may of course have been that they just didn't want a severely myopic little sister infringing on their football games. And so, while I longed to play football with the other kids, my mom would often find me reading a book or seated in front of a puzzle in the shadow of my grand piano, almost always sipping a cup of lemon and honey tea.

The day the world appeared significantly clearer wasn't when I had the eye operations that would correct my vision. It became clearer one Friday when my father arrived home from the school where he taught geography and biology. He would later go on to become the headmaster.

I was about five or six years old when my father arrived at our garden gate one day, carrying a large geographic globe. It was wonderfully constructed, the kind of didactic tool with the world properly tilted to illustrate Earth's true north. Ernő and András joined me as I ran to the gate to greet my father; we all wanted to see what this strange object was.

The globe was a gift he received for refereeing a local football game. I would often watch him on weekends. His mastery and runs on the field during matches made me proud of him. My brothers soon lost interest that day and headed outside with their globe of choice, the football!

My father spent most of that weekend discussing the different countries around the world with me. Looking back, I swear it was in that instant that the little travel flame started to burn in my belly. My mother would look up at us from time to time, a confident smile on her face. She was busy preparing her special 'floating islands' dessert, just for me. We spent that entire weekend spinning the globe around and around. My father would patiently explain each country in great detail. Some of the continents had mountain ranges raised in relief and my little hands flitted over the surface of each one with great care. Who would have thought that years later my travels would crisscross many of those oceans and continents?

My dad smiled at my wide eyes while he explained that not everyone who lived on the planet could speak Hungarian. Even when American movies like *Grease* and *Back to the Future* came to my small town, they were all dubbed in Hungarian. He used the story of the Tower of Babel to explain different languages to me. Neither of us expected at the time that I would go on to work in more than twenty countries and learn five languages in my career. I even called seven of those countries 'home' for varying lengths of time.

My attempt to master a sixth language, Mandarin, is stalled at "able to converse" level. My pronunciation is sometimes a source of great merriment to those within earshot. It does not stop me from trying.

Poor pronunciation has never stopped me from doing my best to communicate, and when my languages fail me, I fall back on a mixture of charades and laughter to get my point across.

Change Matters is written for change leaders, practitioners, CEOs, and anyone else helping their teams to change course in a constant sea of transition. I have tried hard to demystify the jargon. You will often hear me express the following quote: *"Change management is common sense with a structure. It is common sense but unfortunately not commonly practised."*

This book is divided into ten chapters, covering the most frequent change-related issues I have found during my current career. Where possible I have used case studies from my experiences to illustrate a problem together with its solution. While every business is unique, similar change management issues often occur.

I urge you to read this book with an open mind and build on your inner wisdom as you imagine yourself in the work and adventure scenarios I describe. Drawing upon real-life experiences, insightful anecdotes and practical recommendations, throughout these pages, I will navigate the twists and turns of life's ever-changing paths, seeking to understand the essence of change and how it can empower us. Change is a catalyst for resilience, growth, and self-discovery. I would be delighted if you were able to add to your change management repertoire some of my insights and recommendations. You will also find a summary of key learnings at the end of every chapter and additional resources by following the links on my website, www.margittakacs.com.

Welcome to Change Matters – My stories about taming the corporate jungle and leading transformation, where the journey of transformation really begins!

Margit

Fight or Flight in the Quicksand

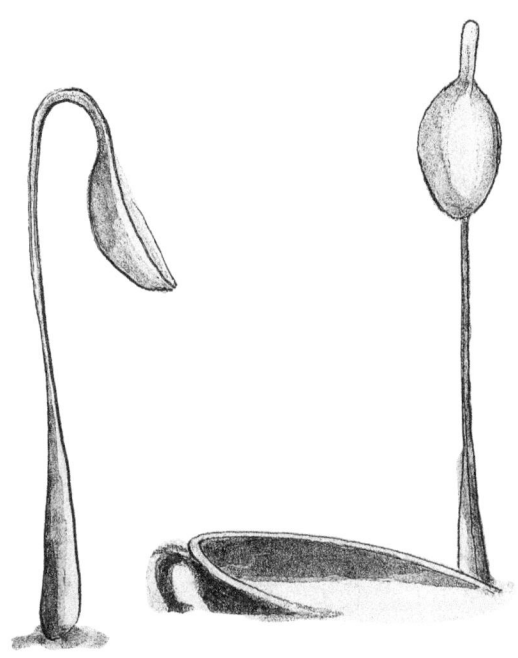

THE POWER OF ASSESSING OUR STAKEHOLDERS

"Seek first to understand, then to be understood."
– Stephen Covey

One of the traits great change leaders possess is the ability to remain calm and rational in the face of danger. If you're raising your eyebrows at the mention of *'danger'* in this sentence, please bear with me.

When we are faced with danger our sympathetic nervous system is triggered, initiating a 'fight or flight' response in our bodies. Researchers say this is a leftover legacy of our evolution when we really did have to fight or run to ensure our survival. The fight or flight response does some amazing things inside our bodies. The hypothalamus sends signals releasing adrenaline and other stress hormones into our bloodstream. This causes our heart rate to increase and our blood pressure to rise. Our breathing changes too. We start breathing rapidly, ensuring that there is enough oxygen for our muscles in case we have to run or fight.

If you're wondering what all of this has to do with change management then wonder no more. As smart as our bodies are, we still respond to stress today in the same way as our ancestors did when they faced sabre-toothed tigers.

As change managers, it's our responsibility to lead organisational changes that affect multiple stakeholders. Our work influences the overall success or failure of our organisations. This important work comes with a certain amount of adrenaline and stress. We're under pressure to meet deadlines, manage competing interests, and navigate uncertainty. I have found that one of the most challenging aspects of being a change management practitioner is having to deal with change resistors. Resistance can lead to conflicts, delays, and lots of added stress, all of which can trigger the sympathetic nervous system's fight or flight response. Our bodies cannot differentiate between the danger of being eaten alive by a lion and the stress of dealing with large-scale retrenchments or an acrimonious merger or acquisition.

In my change management practice, there have been occasions where my client's senior management teams have themselves been terrified of facing the staff, they are responsible for. Their 'flight' response nudged them to abdicate the entire change initiative to someone or anyone else. Just as long as they didn't have to face the 'danger' of explaining the required changes to their teams. Others have displayed a 'fight' response, belligerently blaming affected staff for retrenchments or downsizing. Neither response is particularly helpful in a change management process.

I have a great fight or flight story that also perfectly illustrates the correct way to handle high-pressure negotiations. This happened to me on one of my trips to the Philippines. My good friend Nicoline and I were in real life-threatening danger. Our adrenaline-pumped fight or flight reflexes were in a full surge. If it were not for the instinctive negotiating skills of our driver, I fear our lives would have been in jeopardy.

Here is what happened:

I knew Nicoline wouldn't hesitate to join me on another of my worldly adventures. I was well into my third year at our office in Singapore and I was making sure to exploit the country's central location to explore every corner of the region. I had visited the Philippines previously and I badly wanted to go again. Little did I know, as we set out on our trip over the Chinese New Year holiday of 2006, what would await us on our arrival.

Our mission was to visit the hot springs near an active volcano called Mount Pinatubo. The volcano is situated on the northern island of Luzon, right where the three provinces of Zambales, Tarlac, and Pampanga meet.

On the fourteenth of June 1991, almost exactly fifteen years before our trip, the Philippine emergency services were focused on a rapidly approaching typhoon. They named the approaching front Typhoon Yunya, and went about their usual precautionary preparations. They were not unduly worried. They had lived through many typhoons before. The locals were used to barricading their homes during storm season. This time however, geologists on a different part of the island failed to raise sufficient warning about a second, even more deadly natural disaster that was about to occur.

Just as Typhoon Yunya made landfall, the Pinatubo volcano erupted. The combination of ash and bucketing rain was lethal. Over 1,000 people lost their lives in that double catastrophe and the region had never quite recovered from the devastation. It was to this place that we were headed. A group of our friends bumped into us at the departure gate in Singapore. They were also headed to the Philippines, but they planned to visit the Manila nightlife, a far cry from the adventure we had planned.

Nicoline and I hired a minibus-like vehicle known locally as a jeepney on our last day. If you have been to the Philippines, you will almost certainly have seen these colourfully decorated jeepneys rushing from place to place. They are the main form of public transport and are synonymous with Filipino culture. Early jeepneys were cobbled together from surplus army Jeeps left behind by the United States military (hence their name), modern versions have none of the wartime Jeeps' off-road ability. Our driver had brought along a friend who would act as our guide.

The jeepney's lack of off-road ability was nearly our downfall. Nicoline and I were in high spirits as we headed to Sapang Bato to go and see the volcano. We put our driver's constant warnings about how dangerous the area was down to the fact that he didn't want to drive the long distance from our hotel to the volcano. We paid the premium he asked, threw our backpacks into the vehicle ready for the flight home later, and set off on our adventure with a lurch and a grinding of gears. Young and 'bulletproof', our only concern was that we hadn't brought enough sunblock for our journey.

The sun baked down and the jeepney's spartan interior didn't even have a working fan, let alone air-conditioning. We rolled the canvas sides up to encourage airflow, but even that did little to dry the sweat that was running down our backs.

We eventually arrived at the entrance to the national park where we had to buy our permit. We were early. The jungle insects buzzed loudly in our ears for hours before an official eventually turned up on a noisy little motorbike.

He greeted us with a faux-friendly show of perfect teeth as he processed our permit request, but he didn't hold the facade for long. By the time he had finished taking our money, he had completely given up on trying to smile.

"An American was killed inside the park last year," he said in a sombre voice, nodding in the direction of the volcano.

Nicoline and I looked at each other. Did we want to do this? We had travelled too far to turn back now. The area was a wasteland of dried lava, interspersed with gorgeous flowers and greenery trying to regain a foothold after the volcanic explosion. Signs of the eruption were still in evidence everywhere.

Our mood had recovered after the strange episode at the ticket hut. Even our driver was smiling and bobbing his head as Nicoline and I sang the words to *Love Generation*, the Bob Sinclair Football World Cup song from that year. Another jeepney laboured into view, stopping a little way away from us.

"Stay inside, stay low," said our guide.

The atmosphere had suddenly turned icy. I could sense danger all around us. Even the insects seemed to have stopped their incessant noise. I tried to see what was going on. The driver of the other car was having a heated argument with our guide. He kept stabbing his finger in our direction. Men piled out of the car. They were dressed in what looked like camouflage gear. One of the men reached back into the car and casually lifted out a rifle.

Nicoline and I shrunk lower into the seat. I could just see our driver over the doorsill. He seemed to be content to let the other man do all the talking. He reached into his pocket and retrieved a small package of betel nuts, listening intently and nodding his head as the other man's voice rose again, he popped one of the nuts into his mouth. The man with the rifle was now pointing the barrel directly at us. I was sure we were about to be kidnapped or worse.

Eventually, the yelling stopped, and the rifle disappeared from view. Our driver offered betel nuts to the men who solemnly reached into the package. It seemed that the occupants of the other car were from a local village. They were claiming that we were on their land illegally. Our driver showed them the permit we had purchased from the park authorities. The other man grabbed the paper and threw it to the ground without glancing at it. Our driver calmly continued chewing on the betel nut. His gaze locked onto a point somewhere between the other man's feet. I could tell from the stiffness of his back that he was alert and assessing the situation. Eventually the other man finished his tirade.

I couldn't understand the words he was using, but from his tone I sensed that our driver was being respectful, almost deferential towards the strangers. He told us later that he had sympathised with the villager's troubles. It seemed that their village had all but been wiped out in the eruption catastrophe, and they were still fighting for their survival. Against all odds, the two men seemed to have reached a solution.

I read somewhere that betel nuts are shared during Filipino social gatherings as a symbol of friendship and hospitality. I would find out later about the mythical Filipino god Bantugan who would transform into a fierce and unbeatable warrior after chewing betel nuts. I was not sure if our driver was aiming for friendship and hospitality or hoping to change into an unbeatable warrior. Somehow his betel nuts helped the situation.

Our driver gestured towards our jeepney, and with outstretched arms indicated an imaginary line. He then pointed to the other vehicle and with his palms outstretched, he signalled a 'stop' motion, indicating that we would not cross this point.

"We won't be going to the volcano today," our driver said, clambering back into the jeepney. That made me very happy as visiting a volcano was now the last thing on my mind.

With a clatter and more grinding of gears, he turned our vehicle around and we headed off in the direction from which we had come. We couldn't stop talking about what had just happened. Our driver filled us in on the details of the altercation. He explained that since the eruption tourists had stopped visiting the area and work for guides was scarce. He told us that he had offered to bring them tourists from the city. I told him that it was only by his staying calm and rational that he was able to extricate us from the situation safely and without anyone getting hurt.

He grinned and said, "It was all because of the [1]Nganga!"

In places volcanic ash had formed a particularly treacherous quicksand. It was tricky to see where the patches of quicksand lay, as the surface had dried to a uniform brown colour in the sun. It was only when one was right on top of the stuff that you realised it was there. There were two narrow tracks that our driver was doing his best to stay on, and he was driving as quickly as conditions allowed. The rifle-bearing villagers could change their minds at any minute. All of us felt happy to be getting out of there. But the drama was not over yet.

We were still so caught up in the shock of what had just happened that we did not notice our jeepney starting to slide off the road. Our driver spun the steering wheel helplessly, but it did no good. In surreal slow motion, we skidded down a small embankment and into a bath of quicksand. We felt the jeepney slowly sink into the quagmire until it came to rest on its axles. The vehicle jack was useless in that situation. The sun rose a little higher into the sky.

Nicoline looked at me. "What do we do now?"

"Now we walk," said the guide. "The driver will stay with the car."

---

[1] *Nganga is the colloquial term for betel nut.*

We made our way along the track, discussing our options. The youthful invulnerability that had protected me during all my previous adventures was fading fast. There was no way we were going to get to the airport for our flight back to Singapore that evening. Then our guide spotted a homestead, about halfway up an impossibly green hillside. He didn't have to speak. We picked up the pace and headed toward the brightly coloured house. I am not sure how far we walked, but the house just didn't seem to be getting any closer. Eventually, we heard a dog barking, and a scruffy mixed breed came running down the drive to greet us. A family was seated around a table on the veranda in the shade on that beautiful Sunday. The elderly couple listened intently as the guide explained our predicament. The woman gestured to us. It was an invitation to come clean up. We gratefully accepted the bucket of water. When we were done, we were offered tea and deliciously cool water to drink. We were relieved when our guide explained that the elderly man would take us directly to the airport.

After thanking his wife, Nicoline and I found ourselves perched high on a pile of palm leaves with our backpacks, bouncing along on the back of a vintage truck.

When we met up with our Manila-exploring friends at the airport, we found it impossible to explain our adventure.

"You guys only went sightseeing?" our friend asked incredulously. "How boring!"

Nicoline leaned over and pulled a small insect from my hair, no doubt a passenger from the back of the farmers' truck.

"Yes," said Nicoline with a huge smile, "incredibly boring."

A few things have stayed with me from that trip. When we are faced with a 'fight or flight' situation, there is often a third option: seek to understand the other person's situation and then negotiate as if your life depends on it to be understood.

Filipinos are considered one of the bubbliest nations in the world. It is such a pleasure for me when I get an opportunity to interact with their almost always joyous culture; but, as with all of us, there is more going on under the surface than what they allow us to see. A smile on the outside is no indicator of what is going on inside.

I do not doubt that Nicoline and I were in danger that day. We were saved by our guide's calm and respectful handling of the situation. Even after we had left the area, he logically and carefully explained what happened to us from the villagers' point of view. He understood the gunslinging guide's need for survival. And he understood that our only way out was diplomacy. These were well-learnt lessons that I would come to rely on many times in my career as a change consultant. On the flight back to Singapore I kept playing the adventure over in my mind.

'What an experience,' I thought.

Work continued unabated at our busy Singapore office and the memory of my adventure with Nicoline had begun to fade when, out of the blue, I was reminded of our trip. A call came in from our Manila office. The manager there was asking for our help to ease the impact of a major move to new offices some way out of town. Developers had constructed a huge business park with a mix of manufacturing sites and offices. Many of our clients had already moved there and others we canvassed said they would consider moving as soon as they could get out of their current leases. It made great business sense for us to be there as well. The problem he was having was that while his team was enthusiastic about the modern new facility, he was hearing feedback that many were troubled about school routes and travel times. Our Manila manager was ready to tear his hair out.

My boss Amod and I had just completed an intensive new change management training within the company. We both scored well in the final exams and were keen to try out our new skills.

"Should we go and help them cope with this move to the new service centre?" He asked.

"Yes, of course, who better than us?" I joked.

There is no word for stress in any of the Filipino languages that I know of. Of course, Filipinos get stressed, as we all do, but in the Philippines, there seems to be a sense of community and good humour to combat that stress. It is unlike anything I have experienced in other places in the world, but this happiness facade sometimes makes it difficult to dig beneath the surface in any change management process.

In my practice, the ubiquitous 'stakeholder analysis' tool is mightily important. Stakeholder Analysis is pretty much 80 per cent of what we do as change leaders and practitioners. It is also very easy to get it wrong. The stakeholder analysis in my view is what sets great change managers apart from good ones. There are many stakeholder analysis methodologies available, from simple spreadsheets to bespoke templates that cost thousands of dollars. It is in how these are used that the magic lies.

So often assumptions are made after a cursory form-filling exercise and the change management practitioner too quickly says, "OK, done that. Let's move on." The information may have been entered into the template, but without validation, it is all meaningless. In my practice, I encourage clients to spend the majority of their time talking to stakeholders and diving deep into validation, learning the underlying concerns, interests and whether there is resistance or compliance.

What I learnt from the rifle incident with Nicoline and how it was managed by our guide pushed me to always try and peer beneath the surface in every interaction. Every person is like an iceberg: we see them behaving and acting in a certain way, and we may jump to certain conclusions based on what we see. Effective stakeholder analysis should take a look beneath the waterline, and inspect the values, beliefs, and many more invisible factors that lead people to behave the way they do. This can only be achieved with the utmost trust that the responses remain strictly confidential. No one is going to let you look below the surface if they don't trust you implicitly with what they are allowing you to see.

When my boss and I arrived in Manila, we discovered that Emilio had done most things correctly. Emilio was a big personality type of guy, open-minded, flamboyant, and seemingly extremely happy in his role. He had checked all the boxes in his change management toolkit. It looked like he understood what was in and out of scope. In his group sessions, he helped his team develop a well-thought-out, short but accurate statement detailing the changes the move to a new operations centre would bring. His team seemed to know that more efficient routing and being neighbours with our biggest customers would positively impact the business, and them.

Emilio also looked at the shared needs of his team. He had discussed and understood their vision for the future. He received enthusiastic nods and smiles and promises of compliance. So, what was going wrong? Why the lack of engagement? That was what my boss and I were there to find out.

We invited the entire Manila operations team to a special two-day workshop. We had a conference room set up with island tables that accommodated groups of four or five people each. The usual workshop rules were applied. All mobile phones were to be muted. As befitted our bouncy, exuberant Filipino team, any rule transgressions would be 'rewarded' with fun forfeits. For example, if someone was caught breaking a rule like coming back to the plenary late or having their phones going off, that individual would be asked to entertain the group with a joke, a song, or a dance.

My boss and I were keen to 'break the ice' and get the group relaxed enough to participate fully in the session. The 'forfeits' were also designed to keep group energy levels high. We had a lot to get through in the two days. Of course, our happy, flamboyant Filipino team took things to the extreme. After our very first break, I was standing in the front of the room wondering where everyone was. They had all been warned about the 'penalties' to be imposed if they were late for the session, what on earth could be going on?

At the last possible second, they came bursting through the doors. I had been well and truly pranked. The group had tiptoed back from their break and gathered in complete silence just outside the room. When they burst through the doors the noise was indescribable. Each group was chanting or singing a song at the top of their voices. I was relieved and joined in the laughter. Secretly, I was pleased. We had achieved our goal of keeping the energy up all right. Yet, I couldn't shake my premonition that underneath the bubbly surface, there was something else going on, something that we needed to understand before the big move to the new operations centre.

We got busy reviewing everything that Emilio had started on the project. I especially took a long look at Emilio's stakeholder analysis template. We went through every entry, each person's mindset, current and desired. Were they resisting, sitting on the fence, being supportive or committed? and then we developed an influencing strategy to bring people on board. I am sure this sounds like common sense, but from my experience, much of change management is about common sense that is not commonly practised. Emilio was a bit taken aback when he too was dragged into a stakeholder interview by Amod.

For the rest, my mission was to see underneath 'the iceberg' and behind the smiles and joviality on each of Emilio's stakeholder analysis reports, trying to truly understand each of the people that he had interviewed.

During this process, I attempted to see behind the assumptions he had made along the way. With Emilio's agreement, I took the time to validate several of his interviews by confidentially talking to people he had already seen. A dynamic I have encountered several times over the years when conducting workshops like this is that the introverted types are less likely to volunteer information. While the group sessions were underway, I would quietly ask one member from a table group to join me in private. It was during one of these one-on-one stakeholder sessions that things escalated wildly.

A female staff member entered the room I was using for these sessions and immediately saw me as a sabre-toothed tiger coming to get her. Her "fight or flight" response kicked in and her adrenaline was surging as she accused me of attempting to ruin her family. I took a leaf from my Filipino guide's book and listened calmly to her rant. I didn't have the luxury of a betel nut to chew, so I sipped calmly from my glass of water. When she was done, her chest heaving and her dark eyes piercing daggers in my direction, I uncovered the cause of her fear. It turned out that her husband worked nightshift and the poor woman was already tasked with raising their two young children pretty much on her own. This included getting them to school by bus before she could make her own, onward journey to our office. After the move to our new hub, this would be impossible because of the distance she would have to travel.

Emilio had been transparent about the move and had even invited all of his team members to the building site to see the facility first-hand. This staff member could not accept the reality of what was to come and had not even discussed the upcoming move with her husband.

And here is the kicker. This employee had been spreading discontent amongst all the other parents on the floor. When she entered the room for her meeting with me, her months of worry and frustration exploded. I was painted with the 'head office' brush, and therefore responsible for everything that was seemingly going wrong in her life. I was the sabre-toothed tiger coming to get her, and because she couldn't flee, she was ready to fight. It is at this point that I should point out that our job as change leaders is not to fix people's problems. It is difficult at times not to be affected, but our role is to help our organisations stay profitable and healthy, and to do so with respect and integrity. This guarantees the best outcome for the largest number of people. As it turned out, this incident was a storm in a teacup. The huge commercial development which would be our new home in the region was earmarked to be served by a dedicated and modern public transport system. The city had allocated millions to the project, thus ensuring that all the people employed there could get to work quickly and efficiently.

As part of our session, the table groups had been conducting stakeholder analyses on each other. This is a strategy I use, not so much to gather the hard data, but for the involved teams to understand why the change was needed, and where everyone sat on the continuum. Of course, we excluded no one from the exercise. Emilio was one of the first to volunteer. All of the data from these sessions were stored in a secure folder on a computer; only this time it wasn't. I am not sure who was responsible for the lapse, but a password had not been set and anyone could access the folder. As luck would have it, Emilio was looking for a report and stumbled across his stakeholder analysis.

On the last day, as Emilio was thanking us and his team for their participation, he held up a green folder. "Does anyone know what this is?" He asked. The group enthusiastically admitted that they had no clue. "It's my stakeholder analysis!" he said to applause and laughter. "Do you want to know what it says?" Again, the group enthusiastically shouted in the affirmative. "It says that I am a resistor and that I do not want to move to the new hub!" At this point, Emilio was no longer able to contain his laughter. "Who do you think signed the lease? It was me!"

Done right, stakeholder analyses makes our task as change professionals easier. But they are easy to get wrong. When faced with "fight or flight", remember there is a third option; negotiation through seeking to first understand. It is easy to be carried away by assumptions that can lead to horrible misunderstandings. Validating is a must.

As a business owner or change manager you are sometimes going to be placed in situations of huge stress. You must develop strategies to manage this effectively. Your teams are relying on you to act as a voice of reason, even while those around them may be freaking out. While it's natural to feel anxious or stressed when driving significant change initiatives, allowing these emotions to take over never leads to anything good. It is super important to find techniques to manage the stress that work for you.

It is only by staying calm, cool and collected that change managers can keep their teams focused on the goals of the change initiative, manage resistance effectively, and mitigate the negative effects of stress on themselves and those impacted by the project.

Summary of key learning points

- Plan and prepare: Before conducting your stakeholder interviews, it's important to prepare properly. This involves lots of thinking about which stakeholders you need to approach, developing a structured list of questions to ask, and of course, ensuring that you have the necessary resources and tools to conduct the interviews.

- Establish trust and rapport: Effectively connecting with stakeholders is probably the most important part of the entire stakeholder analysis process. Take the time to introduce yourself and your agenda, make sure that the person being interviewed understands the purpose of the interview, and create a relaxed and comfortable environment.

- Listen attentively, stay calm and avoid arguing any point: Active listening is essential to successful stakeholder analysis interviews. We are not there to try and convince or influence. Listen carefully to the stakeholder's responses, ask open-ended questions to encourage them to elaborate, and try to avoid interrupting or passing on your own views or influencing their ideas. Listen for what is not being said.

- Look beyond the mask: A smiling, happy demeanour is not always what it looks like on the surface. Many cultures will avoid disrespecting and disappointing you, so they will tell you what they think you want to hear.

Trouble in Paradise

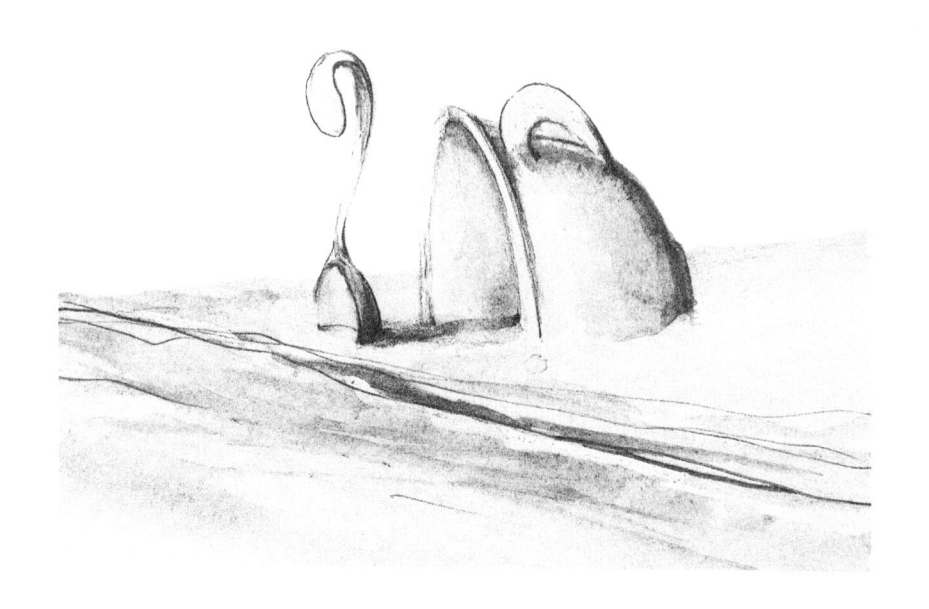

NAVIGATING THE CULTURAL LANDSCAPE

"In a world where we are all connected, it is more important than ever to make sure we understand each other."
– Oprah Winfrey

Bali, Indonesia, is an island of contrasts. Rich in culture and customs. It is an exotic mystery destination nearly everyone wishes to visit at least once; and with good reason, as there are so many things to explore and experience! Breathtakingly scenic, Bali is also a potential nightmare for a young project manager like me in 2007. Local expertise is central to the success of nearly every project undertaken away from home, and my story of a program I was tasked with organising, illustrates this in an amusing way.

As with my other projects in the Asia Pacific region, the audience was large and important. Sometimes my stakeholder groups are small, but they are always important; and the expected outcome was generally the same; pressure on me not to mess up. This story, while not technically a change-related story, had an important learning moment for me about cross-cultural differences in the work context, which has served me well in my change practice over the years. That is why I have included it in this book. Attendees would be flying to Bali from forty countries in the region. The logistics of coordinating travel from far-off places as tiny as Samoa and as large as China would be a giant task in its own right, and luckily was outside of my portfolio at the time.

This however was not the sole challenge. We were used to large-scale programs, bringing people together, coordinating them, and making sure they would have an experience that would leave them with stories that they would go on to tell their grandchildren. This event was to be a grand ceremony in honour of the top 120 performing people in our company's Asia Pacific region. Attendees were to receive awards for their outstanding performance and contributions to our company, during the previous year. What made these accolades exceptional was that not a single person selected was chosen by our company's management. Every winner was picked by a secret ballot held by their colleagues.

These were the cream of our multi-cultural and multi-lingual Asia Pacific workforce. While their cultures and languages were different, they all shared the same customer-centric, can-do attitude. Jointly, they had contributed to the resilience that had seen the region deliver great results during pretty tough global trading conditions. When you consider that this group of high achievers was selected from a pool of over 45,000 employees throughout the Asia Pacific, then you will realise how important an event it was.

My deep dive into Balinese culture began bewilderingly long before my flight to the island was even booked. I started calling prospective venues and vendors by phone from our head office in Singapore. It was after one of these calls that it dawned on me. Nearly all of the people I was talking to share the same name.

'This is impossible!' I remember thinking, as I wrote yet another post-it message to a man named Wayan. What made this even more confusing was that the previous Wayan I spoke to had definitely been a woman. What was going on?

It turns out that nearly everyone in Bali shares a version of one of four names. In Bali, people use a traditional naming system based on birth order. The first-born child is typically given the name Wayan or Gede, the second-born is called Made or Kadek, the third-born is Nyoman or Komang, and the fourth-born is named Ketut. To make things even more confusing to anyone not familiar with Balinese family culture, these names are not gender-specific, they are used for both boys and girls. Despite their similar names, people keep track based on contextual clues like nicknames or personal identifiers.

Only after I had learnt this was I able to decipher the mystery of several Ni Wayan's who kept leaving messages for me! Readers will know the importance of remembering names. Attendees at my lectures will hear me mention ad-nauseum the importance of remembering and addressing stakeholders correctly. It shows care and respect of course, but showing courtesy to even the lowest-tiered team member is critical. Often the real influencers are not who you expect them to be. Knowing someone's name is always the first step to building trust in any work or personal relationship!

Learning the names of my vendors and suppliers was not the only challenge I faced organising this event. I spent many hours studying the selection criteria for the winners to ensure the process was fair and transparent. Choosing a winner also means that someone else has to be the loser. I have often seen that awards ceremonies turn out to be not what the motivator management had hoped for. Perception is indeed a reality, and we need to work with its context. This is why having the winners selected by a secret colleague ballot worked so well. My role as a project leader was to ensure that we had done our due diligence as a service not just to the attendees, but also to the thousands of staff who hadn't been selected. They needed to know that everything was fair and transparent.

Bali is similar to any tropical island in that the weather can be unpredictable. What starts out as a beautifully hot day under an azure sky can quickly turn into a tempest of monsoon proportions, especially between the months of December and February. Of course, our event fell right at the end of the rainy season!

But in Bali, there is a saying that for every problem there is a solution. For me, this weather solution on Bali took the form of a *Rain Stopper*. I had balked at first. How would I explain that line item on my expense sheet back at the head office? Imagine my surprise when I found myself sitting in a meeting room with my team of vendors, and one says in a perfectly normal tone of voice.

"We need a *Rain Stopper*."

'Of course,' I thought, 'it is obvious, we need something to protect us from the rain.' I was thinking of something more like a tent or an umbrella man.

I quickly found out that we were not talking about a tent but a Hindu priest who would perform a religious ceremony the evening before the event. A *Rain Stopper* is a kind of magician that event organisers hire to perform a ritual dance as insurance against bad weather spoiling it. I pushed back at this idea of course, thinking that I was being made the victim of a prank. But no. When the entire team stood up and walked out of the meeting after telling me that they could no longer work on the event, I realised how important it was to understand and respect the possible spiritual context in every project.

Eventually, they filed back into the room after I agreed to hiring the [2]*Rain Stopper*. We continued through the long list of risk management items and one of my team casually suggested that we would need to pay the police chief a *little something* to ensure that our conference had proper police security.

---

[2] A person who performs the rain stopping or rain diverting is called 'tukang terang' in Balinese or 'pawang hujan' in Indonesian

"No!" I said, "A *Rain Stopper* maybe, but how am I going to justify an 'ad hoc' payment to the police chief?" The summit was a resounding success. The attendees were charmed by the vibrancy and sheer splendour of the island. They felt validated and that their efforts were recognised. Was it a coincidence that whenever we interrupted proceedings for outdoor activity, the tropical rain clouds seemed to disappear as if by magic? I was just starting to believe in the power of *Rain Stoppers* when I spotted the police chief across the room. He nodded across the sea of people at me and raised his glass in a toast.

I called my assistant over. "That's the police chief, isn't it? What is he doing here?" My assistant looked into my eyes and said, "In Bali every problem has a solution.."

As the Balinese celebrations drew to a close, I found myself outside looking at the intensely green rolling hills around us. The topography was remarkably similar to that which had once been burnt into my memory during another hair-raising adventure trip I had undertaken.

My friend Amit and I had travelled to southwestern China a few years earlier, armed with just six months of Mandarin lessons and a Lonely Planet guide.

"It is now up to you to provide the adventure by sabotaging my plans," Amit joked.

Amit was another of my friends that I could count on to join me on my adventures. I remembered that we had encountered a little girl on our train from Guangzhou who began talking to us without hesitation. Her parents' expressions were inscrutable, to the point that I wasn't sure if they could see us. Perhaps they were blind? I had to consult my Mandarin-Chinese dictionary multiple times per sentence to communicate with the fast-speaking child, and it was a good thing I had.

Just at that time, Amit started to feel uneasy. "We should have arrived at our destination already," he muttered. We realised that our fellow passengers were opening up blankets and unpacking containers of rice and noodles. They were settling in for a long journey. The little girl explained our blunder.

She noticed our confusion, lack of comprehension and was ready to bring more clarity to us! We were on a train heading to Yangzhou, not Yangshuo; a mere 1,525-kilometre difference to our itinerary that we would now have to complete in just three days. Amit was kind enough not to point out that if I hadn't insisted on using my newly learned Mandarin, mispronouncing Yangzhou for Yangshuo, we would not have been in the predicament in which we found ourselves.

I was just thinking about how we adults become masters at building walls between ourselves and anyone from a different culture; how perhaps by looking at others through children's eyes we would all get along better. We always need to be curious and have an open mind, just like children.

I was brought out of my contemplations by the feeling of rain beginning to trickle down my face, back to reality, back in Bali. I found my assistant just inside the venue doors.

"So much for the *Rain Stopper*," I said.

He looked at me sadly, with a look that parents reserve for their less gifted children.

"Ah Margit… but the event is over now."

Summary of key learning points

- Proactively prepare for cultural differences: In a globalised world, it is crucial to recognise and understand cultural diversity when doing business in different regions of the world. Change leaders need to anticipate differences, be sensitive to those and adapt their management style to the local culture.

- Build relationships: Developing rapport with local stakeholders, including suppliers, employees, and government officials, is key to the success of any project. This involves investing time and effort in getting to know people, understanding their needs and concerns, and showing that you care about their well-being and respect their traditions.

- Communicate effectively: Articulating messages clearly is essential when dealing with differences, even when everyone shares the same name! As change leaders, we need to be clear and concise in our messaging and avoid language that may be misunderstood or offensive in other cultures.

- Be flexible: Leaders need to be adaptable in a constantly changing global business environment. This means being open to new ideas, willing to experiment with different approaches, and being able to pivot quickly when things don't go as planned.

Fixing What isn't Broken

DEMYSTIFYING NEW WAYS OF WORKING

> *"Leadership is about taking people where they haven't gone before and wouldn't go by themselves."*
> – Seth Godin

Qantas economy seats still offered plenty of legroom back in 2003. I had opted for a window spot near the rear of the plane. A visitor had left a tattered copy of an in-flight magazine in the apartment I had been sharing. Somewhere near the back of the journal, there were layout maps of all the aircraft in the Qantas fleet. I was very precise when the online agent took my booking. I planned to catch a last glimpse of the ocean as my flight took off from New Zealand, embarking on what I now realise was the very beginning of my career in change management.

The previous year and a half had disappeared in a blur. I found myself in New Zealand after volunteering for a spot with an international student association [3]AIESEC. The acronym stands for; the *Association Internationale des Étudiants en Sciences Économiques et Commerciales,* but I guess people got tired of saying that mouthful. Nowadays the organisation is simply AIESEC. The not-for-profit had inspired me greatly when I was at university and the minute I graduated, my application for a new volunteering opportunity was on its way to their offices overseas.

The institution would also be instrumental in aligning the stars which would lead to my professional journey ahead; but I am getting ahead of myself. There are learning opportunities everywhere, as long as we recognise them when they come along. This is why I want to share this story of *The Peach* with you.

---

[3] *Association Internationale des Étudiants en Sciences Économiques et Commerciales*

I was en route to Singapore, ready to take up this internship that would change my life. Growing up in landlocked Hungary meant I was already twenty years old when I first saw the sea. Seaside holiday opportunities were rare for anyone growing up in my town, and I guess that's why the ocean still holds such a powerful attraction for me. New Zealand's Wellington airport stretches right out into the waves. I had made sure that the booking agent understood how important a last glimpse of the Pacific was to me.

There was no telling when or even if I would ever be back. On my way to the boarding gates, the realisation that I was leaving a happy chapter of my life on the other side of the passport control desks filled me with unexpected sadness. As quickly as a little spurt of adrenaline coursed through me at the thought of the unknown adventures waiting for me when my plane landed, I had a strange feeling. It was like my heart wanted to race with excitement but was being held back by the thud of melancholy.

It seemed like it was only yesterday that the AIESEC team shocked me with their warm welcome to New Zealand. I had arrived in Wellington after a marathon trip that saw me transit through Zurich, Seoul, Fiji and Auckland before eventually arriving in Wellington.

My legs were jelly-tired after being on the go for 49 hours. I was too tired to object as my welcoming party stripped me of my luggage and force-fed me a local lager right there in the car park of the airport. This was the custom, I was later to find out, for all new volunteers. Now blindfolded, and with a motorcycle helmet placed over my head, my terrifying ordeal continued. With just enough time for me to slip my arms around the waist of the rider, we took off at speed. The ride through town on the back of a very loud motorcycle seemed like it would never end. Eventually, we stopped. Still with the helmet and blindfold in place, I was led along a sandy path to a clifftop viewing platform high over the sea.

Were it not for the sounds of muffled laughter and the sense that there was a group of excited people gathered around me, I would have feared for my life. I was not convinced that I hadn't been kidnapped for real. Eventually, they lifted the helmet from my head and removed the blindfold. And then a big splash of the famous Pavlova cake on my face crowned my arrival. A ritual that all the incoming members receive.

The gloriously salty smell of the sea air wafted up the cliff face to greet me. The incredible vista of the ocean rolling away into the night took my breath away. This was my welcome to New Zealand. I have never cared much for alcohol, and beer is probably my least favourite beverage. On that day, however, jet-lagged and pumped full of adrenaline from the motorcycle ride, I offered no resistance as my new crew insisted that I down a second lager. They all seemed to enjoy this welcome-to-New-Zealand custom as much as I did.

I count some of the friendships I forged with this group as among my dearest. We remain in regular contact to this day, but I am still not a fan of lager. After boarding, I made my way to my seat. The airline agent had been true to her word; my window seat had an unobstructed view. The flight seemed fairly empty. I enjoyed chatting with fellow travellers on my marathon trip to New Zealand, but this flight was different: I was heading to Singapore via Sydney to take up an internship. Fresh from university and with just my New Zealand experience under my belt, I had lots to learn.

The flight to Sydney would give me four uninterrupted hours to research my new home. I wanted to arrive in Singapore armed with some knowledge of the culture as there would not be much opportunity for reading in Sydney. I admit I watched furtively from behind the brochure I was pretending to read as the rest of the passengers made their way onto the plane. I was willing the seats next to mine to remain empty and had already claimed the centre-seat territory by passively aggressively dumping my brochures and books there. I waited with anticipation as the trickle of passengers started to thin. The crew were directing stragglers to their seats and slamming the overhead lockers shut. Still, no one seemed to be headed my way.

I was about to celebrate my good luck when a man's voice spoke into my ear from behind. "Excuse me," he said. "I think you're in my seat." An irrational little wave of irritation came over me. I knew I was in the correct seat. I had specifically asked for this window. The agent had double-checked the seat details.

"No, I am certainly not in your seat," I answered.

"My boarding pass says I am in A, which is the window seat."

"Oh," the man said.

He was clutching his travel bag, a briefcase, and a coat. He had to bend his arm awkwardly so he could peer at his crumpled boarding pass.

"May I help?" asked a cabin attendant appearing out of nowhere and speaking in an Australian accent.

"I appears that I have made a mistake," replied the man. "I thought I had the window seat."

"No, you're in the aisle seat, seat C," said the flight attendant, glancing at the man's boarding pass. I began to move my things to give the man a fairer division of the middle-seat space.

"No need," he said, swinging his belongings into the overhead locker. "It looks like you need the space."

I hoped he wasn't a talker.

"They've closed the doors and you have the middle seat free," he nodded at my pile of travel guides. He was kind but certainly a talker.

I have lost count of the business flights I have taken subsequently. Through careful observation over the years, I have learnt to split the strangers I meet into what psychologist [4]Kurt Lewin calls *Coconuts* and *Peaches*.

Coconuts have a seemingly hard shell. But once you crack through this hard exterior, they can easily become the best of friends. I count many *Coconuts* I have met during my travels as some of my most endearing friends. *Peaches*, however, fall into a completely different category. *Peaches* are soft on the outside, like the fruit, they open up in two minutes and share intimate details of their personal lives; details I am sure that would horrify their spouses and friends if they knew.

I find that *Peaches* also rarely say goodbye after an encounter. They will collect their bags from the carousel and head off into their world without looking back. My travel companion was a *Peach*, of that, I had no doubt. Soon however, I wouldn't care what he was, because he was about to school me on why some of the

---

[4] **Kurt Lewin** (1890-1947) was a social psychologist who studied leadership styles

nicest people in the region I would be working in, tell whopping, great untruths!

"You're going to Singapore?" He said, pointing at the Lonely Planet guide lying on top of my pile of books.

"Yes, I am."

"I have a Singaporean client," he continued. "The bugger tends to stretch the truth a bit."

"Singaporeans are dishonest?" I asked sceptically. The casual use of the Australian colloquialism was jarring to my ears.

"Oh no, not dishonest. No, not at all. The opposite." It turned out that my travel companion worked for an American heavy equipment company. He had been working in the Asia Pacific region for more than a decade and had built up a large circle of clients throughout the region. Many had become his friends.

I couldn't help warming to him despite his roughness. He was well travelled and loved his job.

"I have friends in Singapore, Vietnam, Mainland China, Japan, Taiwan, Hong Kong, and Korea," he explained. "The Singaporeans are the worst!"

"The worst?"

"You never really know what they mean," he said.

I was outraged. The connection with him suddenly cooled several degrees. The few Singaporean friends I had already made were reliable and honest, but I let him continue. "When I first arrived, I took this fudging of the truth for blatant dishonesty. Then I realised that it was only because they didn't want to hurt my feelings," he said.

"What do you mean?"

"These lovely folk would much rather tell me what I want to hear than cause me disappointment or let me down."

He explained how this lack of transparency had nearly cost him his job. "I would send reports back to head office, thrilled that I was about to smash my sales targets. At first, my bosses were impressed that everyone I spoke to was extremely interested in our earthmoving equipment. I would report back that my clients were putting my proposals forward to their superiors. That it would be a matter of days before the orders were placed; but when those promised purchases never materialised my directors wanted to know what was going on."

The *Peach* had learnt a valuable communication skill. "I learnt to preface every conversation with a disclaimer," he said. "I would start meetings by explaining that I want to hear their unbiased opinions. That it was their opinion that was important to me. I would spend entire meetings just explaining that they should not be afraid to speak their minds, even when their news might upset or disappoint me."

He said jokingly that once he explained this, his Japanese, Korean, and Vietnamese clients did not have any problem telling him when his bid for work was unsuccessful.

"My clients in Hong Kong are still in two camps," he said. "The younger folk are very straightforward but the older the person I am dealing with, the more I have to be attuned to all the non-verbal nuances around the communication." I took his advice to mean that in the Asia Pacific region specifically, I would have to become adept at reading between the lines when communicating if I was to be successful; and also, that each and every country has its own nuances, so we can't just generalise.

I suppose this is plain old Emotional Intelligence and Cultural Intelligence or EQ and CQ or whatever you choose to call it. In the cultural context of the Asia Pacific region, this important communication skill amounts to much more than 'reading the room.' Listening attentively to what is *not* being said is a vastly different skill from actively listening to what *is* being said. We landed twenty minutes early, cutting our conversation short. I wanted to say goodbye to my travel companion, but he was already moving through the 'nothing to declare' exit when I arrived at the baggage claim. He was indeed a *Peach*. My thoughts quickly turned to how I was going to maximise my time in Sydney before my onward journey.

The next few days were a whirlwind of buses to nowhere, ferries around Darling Harbour, a visit to the Opera House, and a glorious day spent on Bondi Beach with a friend. My favourite way to see a new city is to buy a multi-day bus or ferry pass, and then ride the routes from early to late, getting off whenever something interesting caught my eye. When I was in Wellington, also known to insiders as the city of cafés, I had set myself a goal to visit 100 different cafés. I only managed to check ninety-six of them off my list before I left. I can proudly say however that I did taste nearly every kind of the fabled Kiwi hot chocolate by the end of my last winter there.

When I got to Australia, I figured that as I was still technically 'down under' and as I was only four spots short on my quest to reach a hundred coffee shops, I could legitimately claim my record if I visited Sydney's top four coffee venues. The barista's there were not perturbed in the slightest by my ordering hot chocolate at the height of the Australian Summer. Heading back to the airport for my flight to Singapore, I was not sure if I was ready for the new life that waited for me there. I need not have worried. I would soon be allowed to put *The Peach's* advice to the test in my first big change management conundrum.

The global logistics company I was interning with in Singapore was in the process of rolling out digital handheld scanners for their delivery drivers to use. The innovation would save millions, speed up client deliveries, and improve efficiency. This new technology would go on to become the gold standard for all logistics companies and is still in use today. I arrived just as the pilot implementation hit a roadblock. Despite months of training and seemingly enthusiastic support from the delivery team, the drivers found every reason not to give up using the handwritten waybills and delivery notes they were used to. During the roll-out, they continued to carry paper waybills as a backup in case the digital scanners failed.

I was sipping a cup of tea at my desk one morning, mulling over my notes from a meeting we had just come from on the situation. Out of nowhere, I could hear *The Peach's* voice again. "My Singaporean clients will only tell me what I want to hear." One of the last big events I organised before moving on from the AESEC New Zealand team in 2003 was to facilitate a regional event in Jakarta in Indonesia.

By then I was not intimidated by the size of the event. I had successfully facilitated similar-sized sessions in my home country and Germany before I left for New Zealand. This event would be in a different format this time. Instead of a town hall style affair, I would be trialling a concept pioneered by Harrison Owen called an

[5]Open Space Conference. Around 180 participants would attend from every corner of the Asia Pacific region. The cultural mix would be something of a challenge, but I was excited to interact with everyone.

What makes Open Space Conferences different from traditional conferences is that there is no cinema-style seating with an audience facing a central stage. Instead of the audience focusing on a single speaker at a time, I would have attendees seated in a large circle. The idea is that attendees would have an equal opportunity to address the entire group. Being seated in this configuration allows each speaker to be visible to the rest of the group while they speak, ensuring that each participant's voice is heard.

I was thrilled when the new process seemed to be working brilliantly; but then I noticed that the delegates from Japan, Korea and China refused to participate. Even after I addressed them directly, inviting them to have their say, and even after they had nodded in smiling agreement, they remained frustratingly mute.

Later that first evening I pulled my friend Vega to one side and told her about my hard time getting those delegates to use their voices. Vega is Taiwanese and well-travelled. She drew my attention to what those delegates were used to in their home countries.

"In many cultures, people don't often talk loudly, they consider silence as a sign of respect," she said. "They are probably thinking through what and how they want to have their say. Give them time."

---

[5] Open ~Space Technology (OST) was created in the early 1980s, by **Harrison Owen** [Wikidata]. It was one of the top ten organisation development tools cited between 2004 and 2013 and Open Space Conferences are based on this.

Armed with this insight we went into day two of the event. By allowing proceedings to move along without pressuring any of the delegates into taking the floor, the communication started to flow in its own respectful and elegant time.

I was thinking about my Jakarta experience, and how similar Vega's advice was to the story that *The Peach* had told me on the plane when I took a big sip of my tea; and then the solution hit me. I immediately went to find my boss, Amod.

"Do it," he said after hearing me out.

That's how I ended up hosting a tea ceremony for our employees in one of the service centres in Singapore. It was a very simple tea ceremony. I was aware of how much study tea master's undertook to learn the enormous complexity and significance of the rituals. It was not my intention to disrespect anyone. To make sure that I got the gestures right, one of the supervisors helped me with the right tea appreciation steps. In all fairness, he led the ceremony more than I did, but that was the beauty of what I was trying to achieve, doing it together!

I invited the team to my somewhat simplified tea ceremony. Amod was surprised that I had included many of our senior couriers, men who had been with the company for a long time. The atmosphere during the entire ceremony was one of respect for the tradition which seemed to spill over into the conversation.

Long after my time in Singapore, I came across a study conducted by the University of Boulder, Colorado. It showed that the ancient art of tea ceremonies may have scientifically proven social benefits. The findings were published in the [6]*Science Journal* of 2008. The study showed conclusively that subjects experiencing physical warmth, such as when holding a cup of warm tea, also displayed heightened interpersonal warmth.

The study subjects literally couldn't help themselves. How could this be? Warm tea (or coffee) fires up the insular cortex, that part of our brain responsible for compassion, empathy, taste, self-awareness, and interpersonal experience.

In this respectful environment, and with some gentle nudging, I was able to get to the bottom of the digital scanner issue. Our drivers were fond of their jobs. The best part of their work they said, was the social engagement they enjoyed with the customers. They loved to chat while our customers took their time filling in the paper waybills. Being Singaporeans, they would proudly display the high-tech scanning devices to the same customer who had just signed the paper waybill, and would marvel at the gadget, but be very happy to stick to the old manual system.

After a while, the tea started to work its social magic. Some of the more senior supervisors who had first raised their eyebrows when they heard that they would be seated next to drivers at the tea ceremony were now animatedly communicating the benefits of the new systems, one of which was that drivers would now be able to visit with more of their favourite clients, thanks to improved efficiencies.

Often when adopting new technologies, it is not enough to teach the technical aspects of how a new digital device or new system works. It is important to explore all the benefits of the new

---

[6] participants in the study who held a cup of hot coffee were more likely to later judge a fictitious person as having a warm personality. Professor John Bargh, professor of psychology at Yale University was a co-author of the study.

technology too, so that this is understood. But it is *why* the new technology is necessary that is almost always the most important thing. The most important thing is arguably *WIIIFT (What is in It For Them).*

In the weeks following the tea ceremony, the changes were nothing short of miraculous. We held meetings with the drivers and introduced them to a basic *start-stop-continue* tool.

During the sessions, the drivers were asked to articulate how they saw the new digital scanners working in three, six, and twelve months. They agreed to [7]START using the devices, STOP calling the dispatch team unless there was an emergency, and CONTINUE to build great relationships with our customers, coming to work on time in clean uniforms and collaborating with one another. The CONTINUE part of the tool is very important because when people hear all the things they should do differently (start or stop), it is like shaking up their world. With the continuation of several things, they already do well, they feel empowered to build on what they already do, and the change is easier to accept and adapt to. It brings clarity to the 'how' of the change in simple and relatable ways.

When the drivers learnt that they could solve many of their client's delivery-related problems directly from electronic devices and look like heroes in the process, the battle was won. It gave them a stronger 'why'. To remain competitive there comes a time when every business must 'fix' what seemingly isn't broken. Often all it takes is to help your team see a clearer 'how' and understand a stronger 'why'.

---

[7] Start Stop Continue is a theory that helps you gather feedback, implement feedback, and improve future Agile Sprints

Summary of key learning points

- 'Yes' isn't always 'yes'. And 'no' isn't always 'no'. Take the time to strengthen people's growth mindset and understand all the cultural nuances at play during change conversations. It takes patience and it takes practice.

- Involve influencers from all levels in the change conversation. They come from unexpected places deep in your organisation, rarely just from boardrooms. Identify the innovators, resistors and early or late adopters in your team.

- Strengthen the bond and "seek first to understand and then be understood!" as Covey said. Chat with people at every opportunity. You never know when you might learn something new and what a huge difference small gestures, like a tea appreciation ceremony, can make!

- Continue to do what is good, start doing what is now needed, and stop doing that which is obsolete or is not working. A long continue list gives your team a feeling of continuity and confidence. It brings clarity to the future and 'how' people need to work after the change is implemented.

The Illusion of Alignment

DECODING PERCEPTIONS FOR A COMPELLING 'WHY'

"It's not what you say, it's what people hear."
– Frank Luntz

Bonn is a fabulous city nestled on the Rhine in the heart of Germany. It is famously Beethoven's birthplace and marks the start of the [8]Mittelrhein, a UNESCO world heritage site on the Rhine River.

The streets surrounding my apartment were lined with lovely cafés, shops, and restaurants. I was close to the medieval Sterntor, which dates back to 1244. The impressive structure would often set the tone for my day, creating a special *gravitas* to my commute every time I passed by it on my way to the office. I was following in the footsteps of many generations before me as they went about their business. I destroyed a pair of trainers exploring the many parks and green spaces during my first summer there. My commute to the office, even in peak traffic, was usually a relaxed affair, thanks to the almost always on-time public transport system. Inside our glass-clad state-of-the-art high-rise building that towered over the precinct, the specially designed windows allowed light to come flooding into every corner, even when the weather wasn't that great.

But this was 2010, just two years after the subprime financial crisis in the United States had ravaged global markets and sent many companies, big and small, out of business. Many of the big brand financial institutions exist today only by virtue of government bailouts back then. Those cafés and restaurants that lined the streets near my apartment were struggling to keep their heads above water. Bonn has a vibrant university student population but

---

[8] Middle Rhine Valley is intimately associated with history and legend and for centuries has exercised a powerful influence on writers, artists and composers

even with their infectious enthusiasm, there was a sense of urgency amongst businesses in the city. They were fighting for their survival.

Inside our imposing office tower, the 2,500 staff were also jittery. They, like many in the world, had never experienced anything like this. To put things into perspective, my company had until then enjoyed a fantastic reputation for staff retention. A sizeable proportion of the employees at our office had been there for at least ten years, many even longer. It was the kind of place where once people joined, they didn't easily leave; unless they were asked to do so, that is. By the time we were through the worst of the economic recession we would have shed nearly 30,000 jobs in the USA alone.

The impact these retrenchments had on the morale of our company was devastating. All around the globe, multi-national businesses that everyone thought were too big to fail were falling like flies. Rumours about the next big collapse were doing the rounds, fuelled by the media relishing in that years-long new cycle. I was impressed with the way we treated every one of those affected in our organisation with dignity and respect. Our established protocols were very clear about that. This was in stark contrast to the way this radical change was being handled by some other firms and industries. Of course, while the reason for our retrenchments was understood by our staff, the shockwave still reverberated throughout each of the 220 countries and territories in which we operated. The question never far from everyone's mind was, 'will I be next'?

At the highest level of our organisation though, our capable senior management team was taking action that was both decisive and far-reaching. On the one hand, it was necessary for the survival of our company to cut costs wherever possible. To this end, no paper clip was left unturned. But it was the other hand, the flip side of the cost-cutting coin, that was to impact my life in a surprising way. At a time when our competitors were closing branches and offices, my firm's decision-makers did something none of our competitors expected. They started to spend money.

For us to remain profitable they reasoned, we would need to ramp up our already significant investment in digitalisation and automation. This would improve efficiency, cut costs and help us keep our competitive advantage. With the global economy contracting significantly, we along with our competitors, were struggling to remain profitable in our traditional markets. The contraction in nearly every sector of the global economy naturally resulted in a rapidly declining demand for our services, except in one area: emerging markets. We acted with speed and agility not usually seen by a company as big as ours, rapidly expanding into emerging markets. This expansion was undertaken in tandem with our digitalisation drive while at the same time, ruthlessly cutting every unnecessary expense. One can imagine that this would be a busy time for a change practitioner, and you would be right.

We were not alone in our fight for economic survival. Across the Atlantic, all the software giants were also trying to figure out how to replace the revenues they were losing. With so many of their customers going out of business or freezing procurement, their order books were deeply in the red. One of the big Silicon Valley firms had an idea; if they couldn't sell new software solutions to customers, then what about improving collections from their existing market?

Software firms started to get serious about software piracy with varying levels of success. However, it wasn't until Microsoft managed to get all of their major software competitors around a table to discuss the issue, that their efforts developed real teeth.

This led to a collaboration between the firms that would go on to become the *Business Software Alliance* [9](now known as BSA: The software alliance).

This newly formed alliance quickly discovered that between them they had lost $63 billion dollars to piracy during the previous year. That was the tip of the iceberg. Their estimates showed that more than 40 per cent of all software used globally was unlicensed or pirated. They were coming for everyone with fines of up to $250,000 dollars *per instance* of unlicensed software. Worse, they were also naming and shaming violators using reputational fallout as leverage. We knew we had to act fast.

With its risk-averse business culture, our company's CIO, while *reasonably* sure that all our software was licensed, admitted that he didn't know exactly how many licences we owned around the world. With no cast-iron rules in place throughout the organisation, software licences fell under the jurisdiction of the divisional heads of our four key business units. When pushed, they confessed that "it was possible that their teams could have installed an unlicensed program or two, onto a work computer."

Our company employed around 285,000 staff at the time. Nearly all of them used or had access to some form of computer in the course of their work. An audit had to be done, not just to count every workstation, but also to check and verify that the software loaded on each machine was properly licensed. This was going to be a massive task.

"Tall trees catch the most wind" the saying goes. If the software alliance was coming for the big companies, and we were one of

---

[9] The Software Alliance (www.bsa.org) is the leading advocate for the global software industry before governments and in the international marketplace.

the biggest, then it would surely just be a matter of time before they would be knocking at the doors of our glass tower. We had to be proactive and move quickly.

I remember thinking that the hardest part wouldn't be doing the actual audit. It would be bringing each of our four smaller divisions on board to implement the program. With most divisions' focus firmly on getting through the economic crisis, I had a hunch that I was about to walk into a sea of resistance. Every one of the divisional leaders and their teams were already working long hours and this was going to be a time-consuming, group-wide audit. We would have to have an effective strategy in place, ready to smooth any resistance or lack of engagement, which was not easy when the project required more than just a software audit. It would require the development and implementation of an entirely new way for the group to manage its technology assets.

Reasons for resistance to change are as varied as there are personality types. I have found that several recurring themes come up, even if the change projects differ widely.

We were going to need the divisional heads of our four divisions to put their natural competitiveness aside for the company's greater good. They would have to suspend their individually developed systems to build a new, robust company-wide protocol; after which they would have to manage the implementation of the new procedures and ensure compliance amongst their teams. All of this was on top of the massive software licence assessment; at a time when staff members were low on morale and uncertain of their futures. I could already see staff wondering why their divisional head had asked the technology team to snoop on their computers.

We got to work. Our capable project managers planned the next steps for their specific business units on how to assess the software assets. Their brief was to design simple-to-understand, predictable communication with a reliable timeline for the audit. This was to be communicated to all the teams and it needed to be made especially obvious to all that no one employee was being singled out.

Embarrassment or loss of face is another big driver of resistance to change, especially when working with different cultures. I learnt a lot about this when I was living in Asia. What if more than pirated software was found on an employee's laptop? A public revelation would kill cooperation and would hardly ensure that the other staff members remained invested and cooperative. Each case would need to be handled discreetly.

It was at this point in the project that I got lucky. A tall Dutchman by the name of Geert, some twenty years my senior, was to be the program manager on the initiative. He showed many of the attributes a top change manager should possess, despite never having been in this role before. He was open-minded about new ideas, and exhibited a genuine concern for our people. To overcome resistance, it is fundamental to first build trust and rapport with those affected. If managers don't have this, then they should step aside, and engage with other team members who can help take the project forward. Geert was keen to work with someone like me but wanted to retain control of stakeholder management, which suited me perfectly.

David, our CIO had never been formally trained in change management, as far as I knew. Yet, he was so knowledgeable on the topic that he had me diving for the latest research articles in the evenings just to keep up. All of this expertise at my disposal filled me with confidence that our mission would be successful. Having a change leader in him who knew so much about what makes or breaks a change initiative from a human perspective taught me a lot.

It turned out that defining what this successful mission would look like, would itself be a bit of a challenge. In any program involving a large team, there are different egos, different levels of openness, and even past frustrations and resentments. With this program, we were working with four divisions that differed in size and had their own ways of working. There were different geographical and functional nuances that had to be considered. I eventually ended up with around twelve representatives. That was when the fun started. What looked on the face of it like an easily defined objective quickly fell victim to scope creep. I had my hands full trying to get everyone back on track as they each promoted their ideas about what was in or out of the scope of the program.

Using a big flip chart I drew a rectangle-shaped frame and indicated that whatever would be in the frame was in scope and whatever fell out of the frame, would be out of scope. I asked the twelve team members to individually write what they thought was either in scope or out of scope onto Post-it notes. They were then to come up, present and attach the notes to the chart in the appropriate area. After a time, it was clear that they thought that everything was in scope, and nothing was out of scope. The rectangle on the flip chart was covered with brightly coloured squares of paper.

I looked at their Post-it inputs. These would be the future custodians of the software licence systems. How would they succeed if they couldn't define what the program was about? Geert walked up to the flip chart and started reading out what the team had written.

"These," he said, "are nice to haves, but not essential."

Geert started shifting the post-its around after carefully explaining why he did so, in light of our CIO's mandate to him. There were several notes that he and the team could not agree on and those were put on the frame. They were neither in, nor out and they were waiting for an executive validation and decision. When he was done, our CIO popped into the room to see how we were getting on. He walked over to study the grouped Post-its, showing what should be in and out of scope, and eventually, he read them aloud.

"There are some excellent ideas here," he said.

Our CIO echoed Geert's exact words when he was finished. "Now we need to discuss if we should turn these nice-to-haves into must-haves," he said. The enthusiastic and knowledgeable team members wanted to do so much, and David appreciated that. He listened, acknowledged the ideas but also rectified whether this was the time to act upon opportunities. He knew too well that understanding the scope of any project and avoiding scope-creep, is the basis for any successful change outcome. At last, we had a clear in and out of scope chart that showed us what key items we needed to work together on.

After he left, I walked to the front of the room and stood in front of the flip chart. Looking at the team members, I tried to make eye contact with each one before asking for the impossible.

"Let's consolidate all of these great ideas that you have written on your Post-its down to a single mission statement." Everyone nodded in agreement. "And that mission statement must be no more than fifteen words."

There was an uproar. Every person in the room looked at me like I was a crazy person. Even Geert raised his eyebrows. Why the magic fifteen? Because anything more than that people would not comprehend and would not remember.

They got to work. It took a while, but they got there in the end. My reasoning for choosing such an abbreviated mission statement was simple. These twelve would be the driving force behind this very important program. But if they couldn't each define the purpose consistently, how would it come across to their teams?

Eventually, they reached a consensus - a fifteen-word statement that had everyone's buy-in would be the backbone of our program change and communications plan going forward. We spent the rest of the session revising the core issues; deciding why the change was necessary, the threats of not doing the change, and the opportunities that would surely come when we accomplished what we set out to do.

The program was a success in more ways than we first anticipated. It was no easy ride, of course. It took time to implement, but it was worth all the effort we put in to first lay the foundation well. Being able to activate the stakeholders with the help of a visible and engaged change sponsor was critical. Selecting and bringing on board key people who knew our business intimately was also a big reason for the successful outcome. Each member of my group knew both the people in their business units who would be affected, but now they also understood the 'why' and 'what' of our initiative. This helped a lot in our quest to work cohesively. The successful culmination of the project delivered an unexpected windfall. Instead of facing huge penalties and fines for unlicensed software, our audit turned up something else entirely.

Remember those almost 30,000 staff members that we were forced to retrench in the USA? It turned out that we were paying for thousands of software licence keys that were not being used. We quickly reassigned these assets to our new offices in the different emerging markets, resulting in a saving of millions at a time when every cent was mission critical.

Summary of key learning points

- Onboard and actively engage your program manager as we need to recognise that not all program managers are able to wear both 'people' and 'technical' hats, but as change leaders and practitioners we are there to guide, empower and collaborate for sustainable results.

- Having a solid people and technical plan that can be understood by all is essential and will always require a combined effort.

- Take all the time you need to get your key people on the same page about scope. Even when the project is urgent and time-constrained, failure to get your team fully aligned on what is in and out of scope will make it difficult for any clear and strong change and communication to be carried forward.

- Define stakeholder-specific rationale, not just at a business level but also considering the work reality of employee groups and the threats and opportunities that are to unfold.

The Bittersweet Journey of Bad News

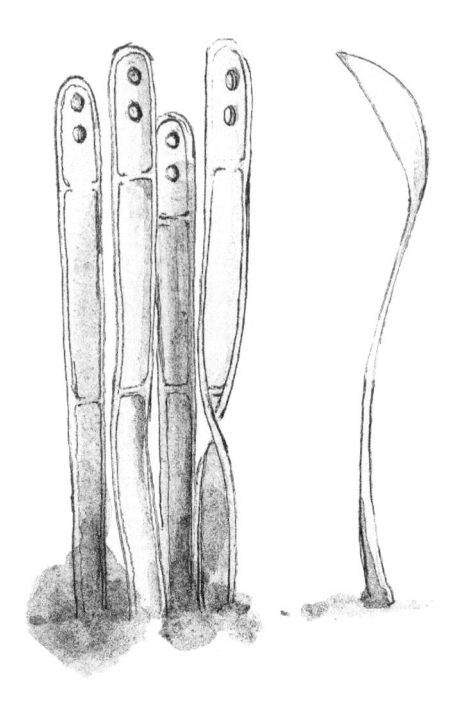

LEADING THROUGH LAYOFFS

"Layoffs are tough, but how we treat people during these transitions determines our legacy. By showing empathy and offering support, we can turn adversity into an opportunity for growth and resilience."
– Sheryl Sandberg

It is the spring of 2019: The picturesque city of Geneva in Switzerland is our home now, where ancient buildings with stories colour the banks of Lake Geneva. The place offers gorgeous views from every perspective. Every walk I take here is an adventure of discovery. This is why I was surprised to discover that there is no proper tea shop in this culturally rich, ethnically diverse city!

I place a high value on the recuperative properties of a properly brewed cup of tea. There are days when I need this tea fix like a mobile phone needs a battery charger. Coffee shops and restaurants are three-to-a-block on the busier streets. There you can buy a cup of tea, perhaps to enjoy with a morning croissant and your copy of the *Tribune de Genève*.

But there is nowhere that really 'gets' tea quite the way I have come to enjoy it. Except perhaps for *a little tearoom* in Pâquis, a colourful neighbourhood close to the railway station and close to my home. It is not even a real tea shop. It is more of a busy bar-and-coffee spot, with colourful decor and an eclectic clientele. I love that even when they are at their busiest, they take the time to brew the tea from leaves. They are careful with the water temperature too. You will not find a bleached paper tea bag at this café. That they serve their tea in generously sized transparent teacups is a bonus.

When my client Max called and said that he had to see me urgently, it was without hesitation that I suggested we meet in this cosy place. From the tone of his voice, it sounded like he could use a strong cup of tea.

To give you some background, Max is a workaholic insurtech developer. He seems to enjoy the crazy hours alone with his computer more than he does interacting with people. Max was quite happy to allow his partners to bask in the limelight during their award-winning start-up years. He was content to shy away from media attention while he ground away at perfecting insurance apps and secure technology for clients.

I wondered what he wanted to chat about since it is most unusual for him to make the trip from Brussels without an appointment. He had already taken a seat by the time I got there. I spotted him in the corner under a bright mural. He was wearing his trademark black t-shirt and jeans, a stark contrast against the colourful wall behind him.

Max already had a cup of coffee on the table in front of him. He was absent-mindedly folding and unfolding his paper napkin.

"Hello, Max!" I said. "What have you been up to?"

He looked up, as though startled at my voice. And then he immediately launched into an explanation of why he was in Geneva. I was used to Max's awkward social skills. In between sips of coffee and torturing the napkin he got the story out. It seemed that his company had invested heavily in developing a cloud-based client insurance quoting platform that was revolutionising his business. Beta trials were a success and regulatory permissions had been obtained. The quoting platform was ready to be deployed.

I was struggling to understand why he looked so stressed. "That sounds great Max, isn't that the tech advantage you always aimed for?" He stared silently at his mug. "Is there a problem?" I asked.

It turned out there was. The new digital solution used a machine learning algorithm that was so ruthlessly efficient that it could replace entire insurance departments. The problem was that it would also make swathes of Max's team redundant. The solution's clever machine-learning ability meant that it required very little maintenance after installation. Max was at once thrilled by the product he had developed but devastated that he would have to lay off people. These were staff who had worked shoulder to shoulder with him since he founded the company ten years earlier.

While social skills weren't his strong point, he was savvy enough to realise that the rest of the staff would also take the news hard. Survivor guilt is a phenomenon that affects those left behind after a catastrophe. It is as relevant in the workplace, often leaving those employees who escape redundancy in as much pain as those who have been let go. Many do worry about their futures after their colleagues leave. It is common for companies to experience a spate of resignations after mass retrenchments.

Max was rightly worried that the remaining team members would become disheartened and demotivated. The flat hierarchy and great company culture he and his partners had worked so hard to nurture would be lost.

"Can you help?" He asked.

I asked questions about the rationale behind the change. I needed to understand the situation from a business as well as a strategic point of view. I was worried about the lack of any form of active or visible sponsorship by his management team. It was like they had built this thing and now didn't quite know what to do with it. After grilling Max for another hour, I looked through my notes.

"Yes, I can help you through this," I nodded.

His face lit up and he grabbed his phone. "She'll do it!" He said, as soon as the call connected.

"Margit will be our face of change."

"Max, Max, hold it. Please tell them you'll call back," I insisted.

Max ended the call looking confused.

"But you just told me you would help," Max said, pointing to his mobile phone. "I told my partner that you'd do it."

"I can't be the 'face of change' for your business, Max," I said. "Only you can." We ordered a plate of sandwiches and a pot of tea, and I started to tell Max a story about a German-owned multi-national client I had worked with. They had a subsidiary in the United Kingdom. The parallels between what that business had faced and what Max was facing now were uncanny.

Max finished his sandwich and was back to playing with his napkin while listening. "It was the most difficult change consultation I had ever undertaken," I stated, "not just because of the technical complexity, it was the emotional rollercoaster we all went through."

My client was a multi-national logistics firm, and like every other business in the sector, they had been caught up in the global financial crisis of 2008. Long after the Lehman Brothers scandals stopped making page-one headlines, this United Kingdom entity was still grappling with the post-crisis fallout.

It was in 2011 that I received the call to visit their offices and meet with their board. I arrived on site to find the client's entire finance team bewildered, angry, and depressed. Their German headquarters had decided to offshore the entire United Kingdom operation. More than eighty per cent of the staff would be affected by the retrenchments. Offshoring to developing countries was a strategy many businesses were following at the time, as they scrambled to cut costs and look for efficiencies.

Taking a long sip of my tea, I explained to Max that the most difficult aspect of that project happened when I discovered that the hard-working management team had, only months previously, won the top prize for achieving the best performance in the organisation.

"They didn't see it coming," I continued. "And it didn't stop there, Max. Fuel just kept on being added to the fire. I learnt that the entire retrenchment process had to be completed in just four months. You know what was worse?"

Max shook his head. "Three of the senior staffers affected, who were only months away from retirement, would themselves have to dismantle the very company they had helped build."

I went on with my story.

"So, far from finishing their careers on that award-winning high and after they had fought like crazy to help their company survive the global economic crisis, these three guys would be ending with a disheartening retrenchment of the very people who had been leading with great results. It was a nightmare," I concluded.

Max stopped playing with the napkin. It seemed I had his full attention. "I understood the rationale behind the decision to go for this financial transformation. Not just because of the external trends, but it was time to find strengths in a new business model. It is easy to be objective from the outside. Yes, this team had outperformed every other division of the company around the world. By a lot. Running an office in London and other cities in the United Kingdom is very expensive. The same office, staffed with highly educated local talent in India costs a fraction by comparison," I explained.

I am not convinced that Max didn't believe I was some sort of unfeeling hatchet woman. The truth is that only a brick wouldn't have been affected by the atmosphere at my first meeting. The CFO had already briefed me on the financial reasons for the closure. I was there to help her manage the process. We needed to act in absolute secrecy. Things would soon start to move quickly, and I wanted the CFO to manage the flow of communication before anything leaked. The golden rule in such cases is to communicate the plans as soon as it is legally possible, anything else would lead to a quick dip in morale and productivity. It was a very sensitive period, of course.

I explained to Max that this was how we found ourselves in a little backroom for my first meeting. A small office far from the plush boardrooms at the front of the building. The CFO had hastily arranged for her team to bring chairs with them into the otherwise empty room. There wasn't even enough room for the seven chairs to be arranged in the inwards-facing circle that I had requested. The CFO and I stood to one side.

"This was my first glimpse of the leadership team, Max. The mood was very bleak," I said. That assignment made a profound impression on me. As I recounted the events to Max, I easily remembered the most minute details from that intervention. I recalled how the management team sat in that little room defeated. Every one of them hunched over, staring at the floor. There was barely enough space in the room for the seven chairs to be placed in a haphazard circle. The circle was my idea. I thought that it would make conversation easier. It didn't. There were long miserable silences. Everyone avoided eye contact. I eventually called for a paper flip chart to be brought in. There was some scraping of chairs as space was eventually found for the chart near the window. There was a strong smell of solvent from the whiteboard markers. I felt a little nauseous as I started to write, first in black ink and then in red. The red marker looked like blood.

"What happened then?" Asked Max.

"I started to write on a flip chart," I said.

"After a long time, the group looked up to see what I was doing. I worked quickly, hoping that I would not leave anything out. I was drawing a rough illustration of [10]Elisabeth Kübler-Ross's grief cycle."

"When I finished, we had an open discussion about how they were all likely in the phase of resistance. Preceded by a phase of denial. I told them that they were all probably very angry and that they had maybe tried to bargain their way into a different outcome. But now, in that little room, it was time to accept the inevitable because their teams needed them," I said.

---

[10] Elisabeth Kübler-Ross described five stages of grief, popularly referred to as DABDA. The five stages, denial, anger, bargaining, depression and acceptance are a part of the framework

I told Max how the CFO had stepped into the centre of the circle of chairs and said with humility. "Gentlemen, I cannot do this without you. We need to have a unified front as we announce this transformation program!" That display of leadership was the turning point. I explained to Max how she led several sessions after that where she put the group into visualisation exercises where they put themselves into the shoes of every one of the staff who would lose their jobs. They understood that their teams would soon be facing a Kübler-Ross' emotional cycle of change for themselves. And as leaders, it was going to be their last and possibly greatest achievement to lead their teams through the stages of denial, anger, bargaining, depression, and acceptance that they would face.

I was speaking directly to Max and his change problem now, even as I was still recounting events from my United Kingdom project. "I helped the local HR business partner write scripts for the one-on-one meetings the CFO and her team would schedule with every staff member. Then I lead them through role-playing sessions to get comfortable with their scripts… I will help you with this, too, Max."

In the face of hard irrefutable data like statistics and return on investment numbers it is difficult to dispute the reasons for a retrenchment program. Equally, the leadership team must speak with a single voice. Max needed to understand that his management team would have to internalise the messaging to staff and not simply repeat words from a script we had written. Is there ever a shared need at a time like this? The organisation needs to survive. The retrenched staff need to feel valued, treated with integrity and respect, and be made aware of the reasons behind the tough decisions that management is forced to make in the course of their work.

Max understood the lesson behind my story, but it didn't stop him from trying his luck one last time. "But why can't you speak to our team?" he asked. "I don't understand why you can't just do it."

"Ah, Max," I replied. "You think your staff doesn't realise that you are outside of your comfort zone, doing this? Your team will know you had to dig deep just to stand up there and face them. They will respect you. More importantly, they will feel respected." Max tried to push back on a few other things too. "But, I don't understand why we have to do it all on the same day," he argued.

"We cannot afford for the rumour mill to rumble into life," I replied.

"We need to get it done before the message affects company morale. Max, how much will the new quoting platform improve your profitability?" I asked.

"Oh, it's not just about staying in the black," he said. "It's about keeping up with the competition. If we don't move forward with this, we will be out of business within two years."

"Then that's what you tell them," I advised. "Explain your rationale, use your facts and show them that you have researched every option. If you are honest and transparent, they will understand. Make sure your team and you are consistent with sharing the news and that you are actively leading the difficult discussions that will surely come. Show them good and not-so-good examples and benchmarks. Assure them you will be leading this difficult transition with the utmost respect and integrity. They may not like it, but they will understand."

Summary of key learning points

- Leaders need to be the human face of change in their organisation. No one else, not a consultant or an expert, can show their people they are there to lead them. And lead with respect and integrity, no matter what.

- Leaders should feel comfortable with seeking guidance and soliciting an external perspective if necessary. Collaboration with people, internal or external to the organisation, is essential to reaching successful change outcomes.

- Leaders are human. They also experience emotions and go through cycles of denial, anger, bargaining, depression with resistance, exploration and eventually acceptance. Being aware of their reactions and addressing their concerns and emotions is the first must-do before they can facilitate the journey for their employees.

- Not every change can be given a positive spin. In an ideal world, we would love to rationalise change as being for the greater good. But sometimes it just isn't. Show that you will be active and a visible leader, that you have the facts right and that you learn from others and can do better together.

Shower Hour and Killer Spiders

FACING FEARS AND HAVING TOUGH TALKS

"See if you can remain patient in the face of anger, understanding in the face of ignorance, and loving in the face of fear. This is the path to miracles."
— Deepak Chopra

I didn't know what to make of the weather when the aircraft doors swung open after a ten hour flight. My face had been scrunched up against the window during our approach to Juan Santamaría airport in San José. It was 2010, my first visit to Costa Rica and I did not want to miss a thing. The grey sky had looked cold from inside the air-conditioned aircraft but when I stepped through the door, warm humid air assaulted my senses. I could feel the perspiration instantly running down my spine in response.

Six months earlier a swirl of changes had come my way both personally and professionally. I was keen to take a break to find myself again and to gain a new perspective. This combination of factors fanned the fire of adventure in my belly which never seemed to go out completely. I had arranged a sabbatical from my ever-so-understanding boss. My parents, along with most of my work colleagues, were horrified that I would recklessly embark on a career-threatening volunteer position in an expedition. I didn't blame them for feeling that way. Even I couldn't properly find the words to explain exactly what drove me to fly halfway around the world to Central America. I tried to explain it in terms that would make sense to them. I told them that I wanted to learn Spanish and contribute to a big, meaningful project, something that would make a difference. I was young and committed to exploring and experiencing other cultures in faraway locations.

This is exactly why I answered the [11]Raleigh International advertisement calling for volunteers. 'This youth expedition organisation knows what I need," I thought. The blurb read: 'The volunteers' mission is to positively impact local communities in the regions in which they operate.' At the same time, I knew that those international participants from across the entire social and economic spectrum would learn self-reliance and leadership. I would find out soon enough that, for many of us, this would become a life-changing journey.

I had already collected my twenty-five kilogram monster backpack from the baggage claim. My bag weighed almost half of my body weight. Orlando, who would become known to us as Nano, was waiting for me as I exited arrivals. He greeted me as though I was a long-lost family member, his huge smile immediately settled my nervousness at this new adventure I had gotten myself into. He had been introduced to me by a dear work colleague, his brother called Paul. And while we had corresponded via email, we had never actually laid eyes on one another.

The lack of familiarity didn't stop my emailer from providing me with a first-class welcome to his world of the *Ticos* and *Ticas*. These are colloquial names by which Costa Ricans and members of some other Spanish-speaking countries refer to themselves, literally meaning male or female. The first task I set myself was to dive into an immersive five-day-long Spanish course. Nano and his family were incredibly kind. Patiently speaking slowly with me and happy to endlessly repeat themselves until they were sure that I was able to grasp what they wanted to share. Even today, each time I hear Spanish, I experience flashbacks to those happy

---

[11] Raleigh International is no longer registered as a charity, however, they still run excellent programs for young people to develop their skills and confidence

moments I spent getting to know this family during the evenings in Santa Ana, a suburb of San José. What a start to my adventure that was!

Speaking the local language, at least a little bit of it, meant being able to connect better with people I would spend most of my time with, work with, and try to make a difference with! When my week with this family ended, I found the Raleigh meeting point, carefully described by the organisers. It was where I was to contact their representatives. It would also be my first official night on the peregrination. I wondered what the rest of the people in my cohort would be like.

In stark contrast to my first easy-going week, this first evening spent getting to know my fellow Raleigh volunteers was filled with awkward conversation. Our group came from widely different backgrounds, and we all felt a little strange as we began to feel each other out. Of course, this is to be expected when a group of twenty strangers is randomly asked to mingle ahead of a leap into an unknown adventure where we would be working, living and sleeping in each other's company without a break. We were all designated project managers and we had just sixteen days to get to know each other while setting up a jungle camp in a nearby national park, using just bamboo and military tarps and many more things I could not even name that would help us through the exciting but surely challenging times ahead.

We were given lessons on what to do in case of a spider or snake bite and how to administer basic first aid in the *likely* case of injury or accident. We were reminded that this was no summer camp when we were also taught how to medevac injured comrades from deep in the jungle, should they require urgent hospitalisation. Of course, this scenario seemed a moot point since we would be out of reach of any mobile phone anyway. Our only communication would be via a beaten-up ex-military radio. That is if we were able to throw the antenna cable over a high enough branch and the fiddly tuning knobs played ball. If we could do all of this just right, then we stood a chance of making crackly contact with the crew at the Raleigh field base.

I am not sure if I had picked up a bug from my travels or if it was the pre-adventure nerves, but on the second night, I noticed my hands were clammy and shaking. My brain was cycling through Elisabeth Kübler-Ross' five stages of the grief. Dr Kübler-Ross originally developed the framework to help people facing bereavement, but I have seen this exact sequence of denial, anger, bargaining, depression and acceptance play out many times in my change management career. That second night in the jungle, as I was processing what I had left behind and what lay before me, I felt every one of the five stages in a most profound way. When faced with a joint challenge, a group's dynamics begin to change. In contrast to our first night, our little band of volunteers slowly began to work together as a cohesive team. There's a belief that there's nothing like shared adversity to foster teamwork. I soon learnt that it is at times like these that the best and the worst come out in people. I remember thinking at the time that this 'picnic' could be one of my finest learning experiences yet.

Julian, the country expedition leader, a weatherbeaten veteran with over a decade at Raleigh under his belt, approached me at the end of the training phase. He reminded me of the words I had spoken that night when we all met one another for the first time. I confidently told him that I would like to live outside of my comfort zone. I had said that I was excited to be doing something far removed from anything I had ever done before.

"You said you wanted to live outside of your comfort zone?" After a pause designed to add weight to his words, he delivered a line that would change my future. "Well, you have been selected to manage our La Cangreja National Park environmental project." I was further thrown aback when he mentioned that I would be assisted by only two fellow project managers from the group. This exploration had suddenly become real. My old friend, self-doubt, entered my thoughts again. 'What in your previous days could have prepared you for this?' My inner voice said. In my native Hungary, we have no rainforests, zero poisonous spiders, and I had accumulated about two days of camping excursions in my entire life. Julian, it seemed, could read my mind.

"You'll be grateful for this jaunt, Margit," he said. A day later, as I was leaving on the field trip, the realisation sunk in that there was no turning back now. I would be spending weeks in the rain forest, like it or not. In my mind, I couldn't visualise what it would be like. Thankfully, the reality would be that I got on well with the rangers. I could understand the importance of what we would be doing, and in turn, my enthusiasm spread to the merry group of volunteers under my charge. It turned out that my worst fears never materialised, and I ended up loving my time there. And that is how, along with my fellow project managers Matt and Gemma, we found ourselves dodging potholes and rocks in a minivan headed for La Cangreja National Park. The park itself was in reality not that far away from the field base. From the outside, it looked like any solid and well-run small national park. The permanent park rangers there welcomed us with knowing smiles. They had seen this scene play out many times before.

To us this was the adventure of a lifetime, to them we were another bunch of volunteers who, while surely committed and passionate, had no idea what they had gotten themselves into. And how right they were! I met Don Bolivar there, the main ranger. One of the most inspiring leaders I have ever met; Don Bolivar was still full of passion for the work he was doing, even though he must have been well into his sixties at the time. None of the rangers spoke English, and my teammates couldn't speak a word of Spanish. I went to work using a combination of the little Spanish I had learnt during my five-day-long crash course, combined with a pidgin mixture of French and English, spoken with my version of a Spanish accent, and of course, charade-like movements. If I still couldn't make myself understood, I would throw hand and foot signals into the mix, creating what must have been the most amusing game of charades ever concocted. We eventually did manage to communicate, and Don Bolivar began our education. He showed us unique plant species that could only be found in La Cangreja National Park. He took us to the location where, together with our young volunteers we were to set up the jungle camp. He showed us how to use thick black tubing to pipe water from the river so we could shower. The fear of the unknown was still living inside me, but it was now mixed with excitement. It was time to return to the field base to meet our contingent of young volunteers.

When I brought the first group over, I proudly showed them a plant that was unique to La Cangreja. Based on my enthusiasm any onlooker would swear I had propagated the plant myself. We were to be responsible for a group of volunteers between seventeen and twenty-four years old. Little did they know that we were just as filled with the fear of the unknown as they were. My strategy was to support my colleagues Matt and Gemma whenever they were out of their depth, and in return rely on them to help me when I needed help. Establishing a solid support group amongst ourselves allowed us, in turn, to confidently offer the younger volunteers leadership they could trust.

Our group was made up of a hodgepodge of youngsters. Some had just graduated from Cambridge and Oxford but were unable to find work because the world was in the grip of a global recession. Others had completed their final year of high school and were taking a 'gap year' before they headed off to university. There were also natives of Nicaragua and Costa Rica, eager to improve their language skills and contribute in a meaningful way to the development of their countries. They might not have had the same means as their Western world partners in the trek, but they brought an incredible amount of genuine care, interest and wisdom. Watching the social dynamics unfold between the youngsters from London, probably sent by their parents to build a little character before they embarked on their privileged futures, and the less financially well-off, socially excluded group, was mesmerising.

The mission was to build a camp deep into the tropical jungle without the luxury of running water, electricity or flushing toilets. In reality, this was only a part of our daily chores. We worked hard but it was a satisfying, rewarding kind of physical labour that left one tired at the end of the day, but not in a stressed, big-city kind of way; more in a satisfied 'got that done' kind of way. I slept well, despite the bugs.

After meeting the new arrivals, I excused myself early and headed off to the room I shared with three other colleagues. We slept on mattresses, and we were using our sleeping bags. It seemed that no sooner had I shut my eyes than I was woken up by the sounds of the early morning routine at the field base. Each evening I would make my way into the kitchen area where thankfully the kettle would almost always be already hot.

One may wonder why a cup of tea would be so welcome in the base camp, but during the night it could get surprisingly fresh. Tea would not just be a pleasant warm drink to ward off the early morning chill, but its familiar taste would be extraordinarily comforting in this alien place. A mug of tea in hand, I would wolf down one of the delicious local tortillas, usually it was filled with a rice and bean mixture called Gallo Pinto before heading to the bathroom. If I had realised, then that my morning showers would be the last ones that I would be taking in all privacy and using plumbed water I would have enjoyed them longer.

All in all, we spent two days at the field base in Turrialba with our younger charges. The time was spent getting to know one another, and learning the "rules of the jungle". We also spent time getting familiar with our tools and coming to terms with our huge rucksacks. We would have to carry everything on our backs, from clothing to food and our equipment - everything for the camps.

The minibus pulled up to collect us on the third day and so began the drive to the start site of our new life. It was hot, I mean a scorching hot thirty-five degrees Celsius. I wasn't sure where I had grazed my wrist. I only became aware of it when it began to burn slightly. I figured this was probably the result of the sweat that was trickling down my back and the huge backpack I was carrying. Did I mention that it weighed half my body weight?

We hiked through the jungle towards the site we were to clear for the centre. Once we reached our destination, we set up camp. I was alarmed at the sight of the graze on my wrist. It had become inflamed and angry within a few hours. Matt looked concerned.

"You need to keep that clean," he cautioned. "And remember to boil the water for at least ten minutes to kill the bugs."

"Bugs?"

We learnt that the jungle was home to a delightful array of small insects, some that the locals called zancudos, a mosquito species that would just leave a benign but irritating itch. At lower altitudes, they could carry malaria. There was another delight, the pica-bella, or horse biter tarantula, whose flesh-rotting venom could consume an entire horse's hoof in a day; and, I did meet a few during my stay! Or the giant ants. These were easily quadruple the size of any European ant that I had ever seen. And they somehow always found their way up on my feet, biting fiercely and painfully. In the heat, I longed to wear cool sandals but faced with a choice between ant bites or heat, I chose rubber Wellington boots. The spiders too were in another league from anything I had seen in my native Hungary. Large, black, and sometimes capable of devouring small birds. Of course, I was scrupulous when shaking off clothing, boots, and my sleeping bag with every use. On our pathways, we saw regular signs warning us to carefully check where we stepped!

Our vigilance did not waver when we turned in at night. We slept on 'basha beds' in our jungle camp. These were constructed from bamboo and military tarps and were covered with mosquito netting. My biggest fear was that a snake would crawl into my bed through the flimsy mosquito netting. Thankfully, this never happened. Actually, in my dreams, almost every night I had one or two sneaking into my bed. In the morning before we would put our boots on, we would check for any hitchhiking scorpions or spiders.

It took us just under three weeks of painstaking slog to build a gravel path through the rainforest. We were proud of our efforts. Heavy rains kept washing away the dirt path that existed previously. Now, thanks to our efforts, the new well-drained gravel pathway would make everything a lot less muddy. We were making good progress with the visitor's centre we were constructing too. The simple corrugated rooftop installation, designed to welcome the locals and protect them from the elements during their visits was already at roof height. That was when one of the most unusual challenges to my leadership arose.

The camp was in revolt. A delegation of volunteers were waiting for me one day. I was returning from the river water showers we had constructed.

"It's Dario," one of the girls said. "He hasn't taken a shower the entire time we have been here."

"He stinks," said another. "I will not work with him again, I just can't!" Keeping morale high during an odyssey like this was key. Homesickness kicks in after more or less the first week. Our only contact with the outside world was with the radiotelephone. Calls home were infrequent, at best only every three weeks or so on our trips back to the field base.

I noticed a distinct change in the group dynamics after the first week. The realisation had set in that; regardless of whether one called swanky Mayfair in London home, or if one's foster family lived in a small apartment in an urban metropolis; here in the jungle, one was only measured by one's character. There is tremendous personal satisfaction that comes from completing a volunteer project like this. We were all getting a big return for our efforts. That return came in the form of leadership learning and resilience. The team needed to work together to get anything done.

This was the core teaching of the Raleigh expedition. If a member of the team was being ostracised, I needed to find out why.

It was not just socially that the boy in question threatened to disrupt the group harmony. His body odour problem posed another issue too. I had not forgotten how quickly my graze had become infected. The oppressive heat and high humidity meant that our camp was the perfect natural petri dish for developing bacteria, or worse! The Chaga bug is so feared it has several names among the locals. It is sometimes called 'the kissing bug', 'assassin bug' or 'cone nose'. In Spanish, it is known as the Chinche. This delightful creature will bite you, suck out your blood, and then for good measure defecate into the wound. Then the disease it gifts you, also known as Chaga disease, can lie in remission for up to thirty years before reappearing and affecting the heart membrane; sometimes leading to death. I am no doctor, but this was yet another one of those little creatures we had to be very careful of!

And so, as team leader, I thought education would be an effective strategy when I dealt with Dario's peculiar aversion to hygiene. Always being sure to sit downwind of him, I started with educational chats. I would go into great detail, describing how leptospirosis, a particularly nasty form of bacterial disease that can be spread from rodents to humans, was highly likely if he didn't have a good scrub after we had been wading in the water, or planting trees. My scare tactics didn't work.

After three days, I managed to catch him when the rest of the team wasn't around. "Dario," I called. "Here, take this. You're going for a shower." I handed him a bar of soap and a clean towel, left by a previous volunteer, and I marched him to the river water showers we had constructed out of lumber and black tubing. It was not a normal shower, and it wasn't an attractive place to get cleaned up either, but it served the purpose. That was what we all could use anyway. It looked like he was going to push back, but I wasn't having any. "Dario, you're a health risk," I said.

He didn't move. I knew that informing, inspiring, or consulting him were no longer options, and that tougher measures had to take place, for the good of the whole team. "Dario, if you won't get in there right now, I am going to get a bristle floor brush and I will scrub you myself". Now it is worth noting that he was more than double my size, yet humble and very kind. Something in my tone of voice or the glint in my eye convinced him that resistance would be futile. Dario showered, and my team looked at me with new respect after that incident!

It turns out that to influence an outcome, sometimes even after you have articulated every reason, explained all the options, and unpacked the alternatives in a clear and non-judgemental way, you will still meet with stubborn resistance, and you will need to make rough calls. Dario was a little on the heavy side. I can only think that he was embarrassed at the thought of being interrupted during his ablutions. . But after doing heavy, sweaty labour in a tropical jungle with every kind of bug and bacteria waiting to take a bite out of you, one would think that getting clean would be everyone's top priority. The outcome was worth the conflict. A freshly showered, healthy co-adventurer is worth any take-no-prisoners stand-off.

In their book [12]*Primal Leadership* authors Goleman, Boyatzis, and McKee, put forward the idea that effective leadership entails utilising a blend of styles, considering the specific circumstances, individuals' needs, and desired outcomes. Without realising it at the time, I was learning how to do that in the jungle. They advocate for adapting one's leadership approach continually. According to them, this fosters a productive and positive work environment. If you are not familiar with the 'six emotional leadership styles' introduced in their book, here's a list.

---

[12] Lead with Emotional Intelligence by Goleman, Daniel, Boyatzis, Richard E., McKee, Annie

Coaching:
leaders who adopt the coaching style focus on nurturing the growth and development of individuals by providing feedback, guidance, and opportunities to enhance their skills.

Pacesetting:
this style sets high-performance standards and expects team members to meet them, with leaders leading by example. However, it may inadvertently create a stressful atmosphere and impede creativity.

Democratic:
leaders employing the democratic style actively involve team members in decision-making processes, valuing their input, opinions, and contributions.

Affiliative:
this style emphasises the creation of a positive and harmonious work environment, promoting collaboration, teamwork, and fostering a sense of belonging among team members.

Authoritative:
this leadership style entails effectively communicating a clear vision and direction, thus motivating and inspiring others to work towards common goals.

Coercive:
the coercive style involves leaders using their authority to demand compliance, often employed in urgent situations or crises, yet potentially impacting morale and motivation. When people have fear, unknown even to them, it is our choice how we want to help them handle the confusion and the swirl of negative emotions coming at them. Each of the above strategies, in my view, has its place and its time. It is up to us to choose the right one.

Summary of key learning points

- Explain the big picture, the why, and the rationale behind the reason for the change: Starting with the 'why', as trivial as it might seem, is what will move people from the heart and help keep up the momentum. Simon Sinek's "find the why"* words of wisdom should always be remembered. To survive in a jungle or any organisation, change sometimes needs to happen for collective survival and for the organisation to flourish, even if it is not always to everyone's liking.

- Face your "spiders and snakes": We, change leaders, also have our terrors and sabotaging little voices before we are ready to be the face of the change for our team members and to support them in overcoming their concerns.

- Be candid: During my sojourn in the jungle, the group tried everything except to tackle the hygiene issue, but passive-aggressive actions are hard to decipher and open to misinterpretation. It was only when we confronted the problem head-on, that the change occurred.

- Dare to be bold when it comes to resistance: There are different levels to tackle resistance, such as education, involving others in a facilitated discussion, negotiations or even coercion. The latter is not ideal, but when it comes to severe, often life-threatening changes, the captain of the crashing aeroplane shouts, "Brace! Brace! Brace!" for everyone to have the best chance of survival. The aeroplane pilot doesn't leave it up to the passengers to decide for themselves whether to buckle up.

Million Dollar Decisions

MANAGING CHANGE FATIGUE

"Success is not final; failure is not fatal: It is the courage to continue that counts."
– Winston Churchill

In 2016, a thirty-two-story residential tower was assembled in New York City using prefabricated modules that were manufactured entirely in Poland. The parts were uncannily similar to the children's metal-parts construction game called [13]Meccano. The prefabricated skyscraper-in-a-box was shipped ready to assemble in the United States. The idea makes sense. Drastically reducing construction time on site saves money. Simultaneously giving busy New York cabbies less to honk their horns about would always win friends with the city fathers. Similarly, the AC Marriott Hotel in Manhattan was built using prefabricated steel modules, this time manufactured in China. The scale of these projects are enormous. Some prefabricated skyscrapers are even bolted together into temporary barges and towed to the site by ship, where they are deconstructed and then reassembled into office towers.

Why am I telling you this? Because *Change Matters*. Throughout this book, I reference my experience working for a global corporation with seemingly unlimited resources, which at the time of writing this book, boasts a staff complement of nearly 600,000 employees. If you're an entrepreneur starting on your journey, you might be wondering if the high-level change tactics I speak about here, are relevant to your micro (for now!) enterprise.

My answer to you is yes, change matters to you perhaps more than most. Take the construction mega-projects above. Those prefabricated steel components are bolted together using rivets

---

[13] Meccano is one of the oldest construction systems in the world, founded in 1898 by Frank Hornby

and bolts. The bolt manufacturing shop making those rivets could be a small engineering works based in South Korea. If that small business was late delivering the rivets, the entire skyscraper project in Manhattan would have ground to a halt, costing millions.

What if the owner of that small engineering firm, realising this, needed to change the way his shifts worked to meet delivery? He would need to implement change. Importantly, he would need to ensure that his team, no matter how small, was engaged and enthusiastic about the changes he was proposing to their shifts. The entire project halfway around the world depended on it. A chain really is only as strong as its weakest link.

My employer at the time of this story had been the logistics partner of Formula One since 2004. In 2010 when this project happened, most fans didn't give much thought to the incredibly complex behind-the-scenes activity that allowed them to enjoy their favourite form of motorsport. Most fans today still don't appreciate the mission-critical role logistics plays in Formula One. Some races are held on consecutive weekends, allowing just three days for the logistics team to move eighty tons of equipment from venue to venue. To visualise this, the Formula One circus may need as many as 300 trucks to carry all the equipment. Some races are held at venues on opposite sides of the world. The logistics company will handle 600 tons of airfreight and 500 tons of sea freight every season. Each gram of this cargo must arrive at each race in perfect condition, on time, every time.

To mitigate costs, teams have up to five sets of their office and hospitality equipment continuously crisscrossing the oceans to leapfrog events. The race cars and more important gear are carried by air on six or seven specially chartered Boeing transport aircraft. The level of detail involved in the planning and execution of this logistical feat is unique. Any change, no matter how small, could impact the success of the event.

This is a logistical ballet on a grand scale. Many of the agents and even some trucking firms are small owner-run enterprises, just like the rivet manufacturer in South Korea. Small maybe, but each plays a hugely important role. One slip-up along the way would spell disaster. After every event, the entire Formula One paddock and all the teams' equipment are packed and gone from the venue before the champagne has had time to dry from the podium. It is a never-ending dance.

Against this 'failure is not an option' backdrop, here is a true story about how in 2010, our USA office, after failing four times to implement a ground-breaking new offering, was able to make a difference to one racing team. It was envisaged that we would use our multi-platform, multi-discipline logistics experience to introduce a revolutionary product to our portfolio. The thinking behind the product was genius. We would use our competencies learnt to develop our highly complex Formula One solution and combine it with our existing and unrivalled supply chain expertise, to deliver any parcel or document, to any destination in the world, faster than anyone else. No matter what it took.

We would have to go to great lengths to achieve this ambitious goal. It would mean using the services of independent brokers, contractors, and even our competitors. A new system would need to be implemented that would allow for foolproof and complex protocols to work seamlessly every time. This meant that we would have to nudge staff who have become entrenched in twenty years' worth of 'but this is the way we do it here,' into a new way of working. The technical challenges were significant. Some airports forbade the handling of dangerous goods at their site. Customs formalities, duties and VAT needed to be calculated and paid in every recipient country. Even if it meant working over weekends and holidays. We would need to create placeholder status for non-existent third-party vendors and brokers until they could be appointed. Our goal was to guarantee at least next-day delivery wherever in the world our client might be.

Keeping a tight hold of all the loose strings when an urgent shipment might already be heading for an overseas hub before its next air connection was booked, was madness. Agents would have to action instructions while they were still hustling to complete information. Every department, outside vendor and agent, would have to work together faultlessly, and many would be from independent organisations or much smaller businesses. Systems would need a complete overhaul to keep track of it all. The potential for human error was enormous; and that was why we needed a machine. An IT system so advanced that it would completely revolutionise the way we worked. Its official title would be 'The Integrated Routing Information System.' We all referred to it as IRIS.

We have all seen the grainy black-and-white clip of Orville Wright's first flight. The aeroplane the Wright brothers built bounced down a grassy field for what seemed like ages before it lurched into the air and made history. Well, the IRIS project was something like that. After four failed launch attempts, it still wouldn't get off the ground. Of the eight would-be 'super users' of the project, six showed serious signs of change fatigue. Another showed all the signs of outright resistance.

While being briefed, my boss dropped a bombshell. "I am afraid you're going to have to run everything from here in Germany," he said. "We can't afford to have you away from headquarters, and you're going to have to stay on top of your existing projects too."

I learnt that I would be working under a senior executive based in the USA, German Valencia, who is originally from Colombia. German would turn out to be a great mentor during my time at the company. I also learnt that I could allocate no more than two days of my time to the project each month.

"This sounds super interesting," I said, my voice an octave or two higher than usual. I asked lots of questions of course; I needed clarification on the scope and impact of the project, specifically which team members would be impacted. Because how would I be able to help create an environment of acceptance if the change was poorly defined?

My boss explained that the project was far-reaching in its impact, potentially touching every department in the company. He detailed how the new software solution would replace order entry and execution modules throughout the length and breadth of every department. He went on to say that the project would even affect job roles, hiring, processes, and staffing levels.

When I asked how many people would be involved in the initial implementation, the numbers seemed staggering. The project would affect one hundred and nine front-line staff, forty managers and supervisors, and the project would have to be run off-site.

My head was spinning. Ideally, I would have liked to conduct a stakeholder analysis with as many of the affected team as possible. Stakeholder analysis sessions are the bread and butter of any change leader. Often treated as a form-filling exercise, it is too easy for team leaders to flip through them, simply to get the job done. Looking back at my notes from my career, it is clear that every successful change outcome has been because I have been able to read the room. The value of observing non-verbal communication cues cannot be overstated. And that can only come from face-to-face encounters. How would I achieve this sitting in an office, thousands of kilometres away, and do it successfully with only a day or two available for the task each month?

It was easier than I expected thanks to using ingenuity, planning, automating calls, and follow-up sessions. I was quickly learning valuable lessons about distance coaching, reading people remotely during interviews, and catalysing change from afar. I still use these learnings in my practice daily. This was long before global pandemics and mandatory lockdowns.

My confidence was shaken after the first conference calls. I realised immediately that the entire project was at risk. There was no dedicated project manager in place, and no technical plan in place either. My starting point was clear. Finding a dedicated project manager suitable for the job would be my number one priority. This was followed by speaking to as many stakeholders as possible to find a change practitioner who I could work through. And then the arduous stakeholder interviews started. A huge scheduling task was made even tougher because of the time difference between Europe and our US office. The scheduling turned out to be the easiest part. The deeper I dived into the interviews, the more I found a complete lack of trust in both the plan and the new system. Buy-in from key stakeholders had completely stalled. The project was at risk of failing.

I had to move quickly. My stakeholder interviews continued unabated, but it was already clear to me that regular communication was going to be essential to rescuing the situation. Celebrating even the smallest milestones, the little wins would be key to turning the apathy tide; or so I hoped.

Despite deploying a clear communications strategy aimed at keeping all the affected staff in the loop, it seemed that the increased communications weren't going to catalyse the immediate success that we were hoping for. Six months after implementation, my ongoing telephonic stakeholder analyses showed that we were no closer to achieving buy-in from most of the stakeholders. My frustration showed in the feedback meetings. There was still just no appetite to implement the IRIS system.

Realising that there was no quick fix left in my toolbox, I stuck to the fundamentals, revisiting stakeholder analyses until the penny dropped. I needed to make changes to the upper structures of the project management team and help them to select a dedicated change practitioner who was engaged and enthusiastic about the benefits that IRIS would bring.

I worked with the project manager and coached the change practitioner. She immediately set out to find out first-hand from the super users how they felt about IRIS. She did a lot more than send out newsletters and hold the occasional town hall meeting too. Her regular team updates with the people most involved, along with clear follow-through on the project plan and her acknowledgement of their frustrations was a big hit.

My relentless telephone interviews continued. From these calls, I noticed right away that there had been a measurable uptick in acceptance levels. Not quite the *en-masse* buy-in I had hoped for, the risk of failure was still there; but the team's focus shifted to the technical aspects of the project. My analysis was showing not so much of the *'why do we have to'* and a lot more of the *'how do we do this'* attention to the technical issues of implementation.

Fast forward to 9 October 2011. It was Saturday, cold in Germany but on the other side of the world in Japan, it was a balmy twenty-seven degrees Celsius in Suzuka. A crowd of 200,000 had crammed into the Suzuka Grand Prix circuit to watch the running of the 37th Grand Prix to be held there. It was statistically unlikely that anyone would beat Sebastian Vettel in the World Driver's Championship. He needed just a single point to take the title. Things were getting a little closer behind him though.

I was still dressed in my pyjamas, a comforting cup of warm tea in my hands. The sun wouldn't rise for another hour yet. My television was streaming images of Japanese Formula One fans dressed in crazily ornate fan merchandise, live from the circuit. My clock ticked closer to the seven a.m. start time (three p.m. in Japan). I knew that across the Atlantic some of my colleagues were also eagerly tuned in to the 2011 F1 championship decider. We all had a special interest in this particular race.

Two days before Grand Prix weekend, a potential 'super user' client had called our United States head office with a desperate plea. He was employed by a Formula One racing team. A small California-based fabricator had manufactured a special part for one of the teams competing at the Suzuka event. It was a do-or-die upgrade that could net them over $1 million dollars in prize money if they could beat their rivals in the manufacturer's title. The Californian maker had all but guaranteed that the performance gain of his specially designed part would do the trick. Could we get it to Suzuka before qualifying on Saturday? Usually, Formula One racing teams send one of their employees with any last-minute upgrades tucked into their luggage; but this time the part was coming from across the Atlantic. Half a world away from the racing team's headquarters in the United Kingdom, but just down the road from our closest office in the United States.

Our team nodded yes, and IRIS jumped into action, thus setting in motion an elaborate collaboration of agents, planes, pilots, drivers, and clearing agents. Everything and everyone worked seamlessly. The custom part was on its way to Suzuka at breakneck speed. I held my breath of course, but the team on the ground in the US did brilliantly.

As the cars made their way around the track on their warm-up lap, I spotted our client's racing car halfway down the field. I am not sure if the part we delivered helped them in their quest. But I am convinced that when I used our communications channel to let the team know that IRIS had just flawlessly delivered on a promise we had made, that little win felt a lot like we had won our own World Championship.

Summary of key learning points

- Engage your key stakeholders regardless of distance: Often, we do not have the luxury of meeting stakeholders in person, and with a little practice, we can still do an effective analysis of their mindsets and change readiness.

- Build trust in the project by having a dedicated and strong management team: Employees need to have full confidence in the project plan. People can't embrace a poorly defined change with a weak technical solution.

- Mobilise an active and visible sponsor, who will spearhead the initiative and communicate clearly and consistently: Other than giving the necessary financial, time, and people resources to the initiative, the sponsor needs to ask for regular updates and commit to practically showing his or her contribution to the project.

- Draw up an influencing map to identify the obvious and the less obvious ringleaders: After identifying and onboarding them, they become the engaged change champions who can help you reach more people more effectively on the path to success.

The Pain in Spain

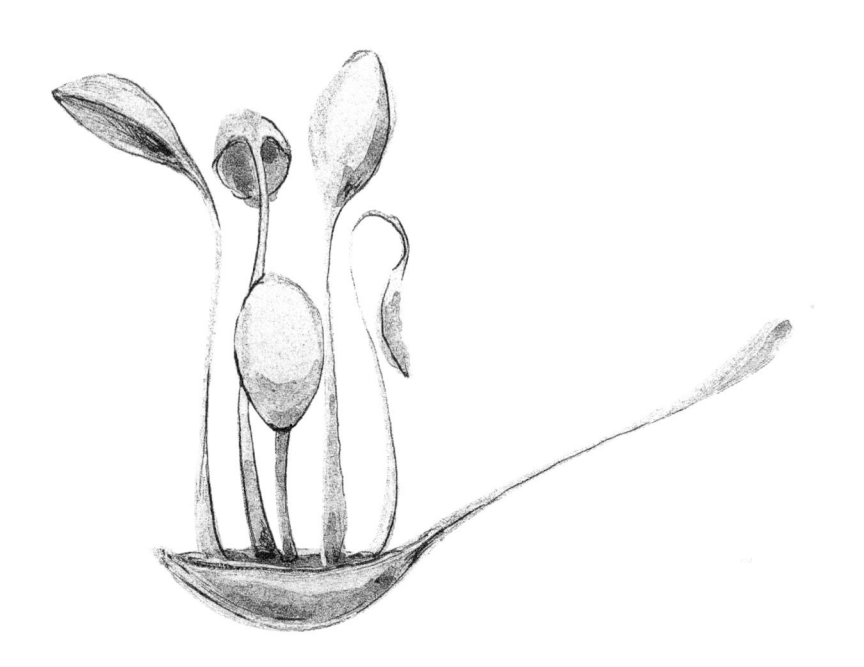

EMPOWERING GENUINE INFLUENCERS

"When seeking influencers, remember that it's not just about the numbers; it's about the authenticity of their voice. Genuine influencers can inspire change, ignite conversations, and build lasting relationships with their followers."
-— Arianna Huffington

Part one

The cold spell that ravaged Europe that winter was a metaphor for the chills still running through many European economies, after the 2008 global meltdown. Perhaps it was because I was so insulated from much of the news while I was in the jungle that I hadn't fully realised how many lives continued to be affected by the crisis. I was more focused on avoiding everything poisonous and too busy practising my 'Jungle Spanish' to pay much attention to global markets.

Inside the baggage claim area of Heathrow Airport, there were bags piled to the ceiling. Overhead the information boards flickered 'cancelled' in a sea of orange letters alongside every destination. I was mindful of the responsibilities the new position within my German headquartered company would bring. I wanted to make a good first impression and arriving days late was not the entrance I had planned. Especially since my last boss had been so accommodating of my Central America travels; but this would prove to be impossible. All the airports in Germany were closed to traffic due to the massive snowstorm. I made my way to the terminal five exit looking for a bus or train transfer to Gatwick. My path was blocked by two airport security officers.

"I'm sorry, ma'am, everything has stopped running. You would do best to wait it out indoors." My heart sank. I was stuck, and so I settled down on the hard floor of the terminal building. It was the night of 30 November 2010. I was scheduled to start work at our Bonn office on 2 December. That was how I found myself surreally drawing on my jungle survival skills in the middle of a modern airport building in the heart of one of the busiest cities in the world. I dug into my backpack looking for something like a makeshift blanket. It was starting to get really cold. Months of living in a tropical climate had not prepared me for this. I must have looked a sight. Wrapped in towels and hugging my backpack, I eventually snatched some sleep.

The £5 voucher handed out by the British Airways man earlier had not gone very far as most of the food places were closed or sold out. The news when awakening next morning was not good. The snow had continued to fall during the night and all flights out of London had indeed been cancelled. My stomach grumbling with hunger, I reached for my phone. My very basic and therefore anti-theft, jungle phone had two functions: plain text messaging and calls. Eventually, a crucial message was sent. My dear friends Maryna and Srini were not going to leave me stranded at the airport. I managed to get onto a train an hour later when they eventually started running, and I set off to find their apartment in southeast London. The next three days were spent anxiously waiting for a seat to become available. Result - an arrival in Bonn two days later than planned and I started work immediately. I learnt later that I had arrived in London on the coldest day ever recorded in the United Kingdom.

Looking back at my career, as far back as my AIESEC days, I feel I have gravitated into the orbit of some of the greatest managers, teachers, leaders, and mentors anyone could wish for. Then there are the two 'Michaels'. The first is Swiss and his name is pronounced Mi-sh-el; and it is this Michel, the wonderful leader that he is, who granted me the half-year sabbatical that made my Costa Rica and Nicaragua experience possible. When I was plotting this six-month-long leadership sabbatical cum life-changing adventure in the Americas, I cunningly used some of the proven change principles I had learnt to bring Michel around to my way of thinking, and he did the same on me. I knew it would be essential for me to prove to him that my sabbatical would be beneficial to the company (I still use my sabbatical story and strategy in the courses I teach today). In the midst of my travels, I learnt that Michel had left the company and moved back to Switzerland.

A new adventure was about to unfold in Germany. I knew I had struck it lucky again the moment I met my new boss face-to-face. I learnt that his name was also Michael, albeit with a more conventional spelling and pronunciation than the Michel he had replaced. He looked directly into my eyes.

"You may have flown home in an aeroplane," he smiled, "but I bet your soul is still taking the slow boat back from the Americas."

He was right. The backbreaking work of laying water pipes and the daily ritual of shaking my boots out to check for scorpions seemed a million miles away, but the lessons learnt and the kindness shown by my friends there were occupying my mind. While my body was coming to terms with the transition between the sweaty heat of the Costa Rican and Nicaraguan jungles, my head was still bathing in the memories of the beautiful adventures I experienced there.

I felt a kind of restlessness even as I leaped into my new role at the firm. Perhaps it was the cathartic experience of facing the unknown and then coming through the other side of an extremely challenging ordeal that made me realise, with some surprise, that I was made of sterner stuff than even I and those who loved me most perceived. I was ready for more.

When my mom asked me about my journeys, I answered simply, "I think I did okay, [14]*Anyu*. I learnt a lot; mostly about myself."

At that moment, I realised that although I had left the jungle, with its Latin influences, the jungle had never left me. A few months later, I was nervously pacing the corridor outside of Michael's office. I was about to ask for another travel favour. 'Dare I ask him so soon in our relationship?' I was pondering. He had already done so much for me since my return. I wanted my new boss to find a foreign assignment. Anywhere would do, as long as the people there spoke Spanish!

"How about Ontígola?" He asked.

"That sounds perfect!" I replied.

I did not have the slightest idea where Ontígola was, and I didn't care. It was enough that the name sounded Spanish. The grin refused to leave my face. "Good, you will be joining the team assisting with the change project in our supply chain warehouse there," he continued.

I learnt that I would be part of the team implementing a Lean Continuous Improvement Program. I was to work with two exceptional colleagues, a [15]Lean Sensei called Ellen who was

---

[14] Meaning; mom, mum, in Hungarian

[15] In the largest sense, a Lean Sensei changes a culture at an organisation and helps everyone to learn how to learn. That involves an open mind and a willingness to change habits and processes for the better.

from the Netherlands and a [16]Continuous Improvement Advisor, a Spanish colleague called Vicente who displayed all of the passion that the Spanish are famous for.

The situation was dire as I was to discover during our commute to the warehouse on my first day there. Ontígola is a small municipality in the Toledo province of Spain. The population is only around 4,000 inhabitants and although located not far from Madrid, the town had been one of the hardest hit by Spain's ongoing financial woes. When the 2008 crisis imploded markets, Spain did what many developed countries around the world did, and that was to spend big on infrastructure projects. The strategy was supposed to stimulate their economies.

By the time I had arrived there in 2011, it was clear that these stimulus measures, in Spain at least, had failed. Unemployment had already broached 20 per cent and the retirement age had been increased from age 65 to 67. Spain was forced to accept a humiliating €100 billion Euro bailout package from the European Union, but even this was not near enough to stop families from being ravaged by retrenchments and out-of-control inflation.

"It's quite hard to get our people excited about a head office imposed 'Continuous Improvement philosophy*' when all they hear about is the furthest thing from anything improved," explained Vicente as we pulled up outside our building.

What had I gotten myself into?

My immediate goal was to blend into the team. The last thing I wanted was to be seen as the 'visiting consultant' from head

---

[16] Continuous improvement consultants plan ways for a company to implement and improve its processes

office. Early on in the process, I discovered, to my surprise, that my limited 'Jungle Spanish' was something of a secret weapon.

Much like the French use the pronouns 'vous' and 'tu' as a formal and informal version of 'you', the Spanish make a similar distinction by using the more polite and formal pronoun 'usted' and 'ustedes' instead of the informal 'tú' and 'vosotros'. For the life of me, I couldn't remember how to conjugate 'vosotros' at the time. It is not something used in Central America, so I kept using 'ustedes' exclusively. The result of this was that I came across as respectful to every member of the staff, regardless of their status. Consequently, I was quickly viewed as a non-threatening member. This gave me the ability to disappear into the background and observe, unnoticed, the corridor talks and coffee corner chats. My mission was to simply gain an understanding of why our people did (or in most cases, didn't) want to buy into the initiative. In the process, I noticed two members of the team and I wanted to find out more about them.

"Who is the older guy we see in the canteen at lunchtime?" I asked Vicente. "He sits with the group every day. The team seems to like him a lot."

"Oh, that is Juan," replied Vicente. "He is close to retirement… if the government doesn't extend the retirement age again!"

One of our shift managers was an enthusiastic young man named Carlos. He was leading a team in an area of operations where Ellen and I were working. At the beginning of every shift, he would gather his team and spend ten- or fifteen-minutes welcoming everyone, including Juan the veteran, onto that shift. Carlos enthusiastically embraced Ellen's Continuous Improvement coaching and the sessions brilliantly. The young manager wouldn't just ask how his team was doing. Instead, using whiteboards repurposed from another department, he asked about their Key Performance Indicators for that day and also spent some of the allocated time discussing the results from the previous day's shift. He would listen attentively to the feedback on the occasions, when it did come, asking what had gone right and what had not. Carlos ran these meetings with a flat hierarchy, encouraging everyone to speak and voice an opinion on what could be done to improve while doing everything right, giving a masterclass in what Lean calls a [17]Performance Dialogue, but his despondent and battle-weary team were having none of it. They would listen, nod, and then wearily drag themselves onto the floor to start another day. Grateful for their jobs of course, but the thought of retrenchment was never far from anyone's mind.

    I joined in as an observer on quite a few of these sessions and became the invisible, polite, and quiet visitor from head office. I noticed that Juan always looked away from Carlos when he spoke. It was evident that he was not at all invested in the process. This was a far cry from the Juan I had observed during the lunch breaks. Most of the staff would bring packed lunches to warm up in the canteen. From the moment Juan pushed the button to pop open the microwave door, his colleagues would gather around him and engage him in conversation. Invisible me managed to get close enough on a few occasions to hear what they were talking about. The topics were fascinating. One woman asked him about suit hire for her son who was getting married. She couldn't afford to buy him a new one, she explained. Juan told her about a connection he had in Madrid and promised to bring her the phone number. Another was struggling to find a car part for his old SEAT which had been off the road, making his commute to our warehouse difficult. Juan not only supplied the name of a

---

[17] Performance Dialogue, also known as PD for short, is a documented and time sensitive conversation between the supervisor and the employee that ensures organisational effectiveness and staff engagement.

recommended mechanic but offered to give the man a lift to work while his car was being repaired.

"We need to get him on board as a change leader. Just look how the entire team dynamic changes every time he enters a room, he is an opinion leader" I said to Vicente, on one of the morning trips to the office. "More than that, he is the true tribal chief we need. Have you seen how people push past each other just to sit with him at lunch?"

I was faced with two hurdles. Carlos was a 'suburb' manager. He was doing everything right, yet his team was not engaged. I suspected that the reason for this was because he was seen as 'management'. Although he did everything in his power to flatten the hierarchal structure during his shift welcome sessions, he was also the guy who had the power to lay off team members and everyone knew that. My other challenge was Juan, 'mister reliable' and a safe pair of hands on every shift, but no firebrand. His matter of fact, but underneath-the-radar approach to his career had unfortunately meant that he had been passed over for promotions several times. As a result, he had never held a leadership position in our company, although I firmly believed he could have done a great job. He seemed quite happy to see out his time until retirement and then go quietly on his way. I was about to change all that.

He was surprised to see me during that first lunch break. I timed my approach perfectly and scored the last available chair at his table. There were a few annoyed glances at first, as his usual group looked at me with "what is she doing here" expressions on their faces; but I soon blended into the background and the table chatter picked up. I was no threat. After a few times, the group paid no attention to me when I approached, and often would bunch up to give me space.

"Do you want to join me for a coffee?" I asked after lunch one day. I had noticed Juan loved to have a coffee if he could squeeze it in before the shift started. He looked at his watch and nodded. I had found a way to open up the door to him.

I spent the next few weeks in these impromptu 'one-on-ones' with Juan over coffee and tea. I listened much more than I talked, and we built up a kind of camaraderie. Hailing from head office, and yet not really part of the Ontígola management, made me difficult to pigeonhole. I knew I had made a breakthrough one day when he asked me straight out, yet in a friendly manner.

"What do you want?" I didn't hesitate. "I want you to lead Carlos's shift welcome."

"Why?"

"Because our productivity, and possibly even jobs are on the line," I said.

Juan was a smart man. He knew that we had to maximise efficiency if we were to weather the economic storm. I could see it made sense to him. "What will Carlos say?" He asked.

"I don't exactly know," I admitted. "He knows we need to try a different approach to do it better. He is open to new ideas." If enthusiastic Carlos had impressed me when we first met, I was even more impressed at how he took the news.

"Juan said yes?" He asked incredulously. "That's fantastic!"

It turned out that Carlos had put Juan forward for promotion countless times over the years, but with no luck. They say that the sign of a good manager is how he builds and supports those who report to him. Carlos wasn't just a good manager. He was one of the best. Together with Ellen and Carlos, we scheduled several coaching sessions with Juan. These sessions went surprisingly well.

"How had management not noticed his natural leadership abilities before?" I asked myself.

Juan was fired up at the idea that the rest of his time at the company would be spent on a mission to strengthen continuous improvement through engagement and efficiency. He readily understood our Performance Dialogue sessions, Why/What/How. In a slightly less structured way, these formed the basis of the conversations he was already having with his co-workers every lunch break.

One Friday before lunch Juan approached me. "Margit, do you have a minute?" He asked.

"I start the Performance Dialogue welcome on Monday. I want to go through everything one last time before the weekend."

We role-played the shift welcome. I made up some tough questions and put Juan through some awkward silences. He was brilliant.

"You've got this, Juan. You are all about getting folk to open up and share ideas. I have never seen you criticise or judge anyone, even when they wanted to dress their son in an emerald tuxedo on their wedding day!" Juan grinned. "I knew my tailor friend would talk her out of the green tux!"

"What's your mission on Monday?" I asked.

"I am going to save jobs and improve morale through Continuous Improvement!"

"Yes, you will. How will you achieve this?" I prompted.

"By allowing everyone a fair chance to bring up problems affecting the shift. I am going to let them discover what the problems are, then let them work through the real reasons and find the solutions to the problems they identified." He said.

"Yes, you've got it," I said.

"There are going to be issues you will have to put to the floor, problems they may not yet be aware of, and sometimes those conversations will be hard. But once your shift realises that those 'performance dialogues' are not there to catch anyone out but to give everyone an opportunity to be heard, so we can all be better-off, then you will have achieved a lot,"

We were quiet for a moment.

"Would you like me to sit in on Monday?" I asked.

"You can sit in and observe," his smile taking the sting out of his words, "but I don't want you to talk. It's my meeting!"

I often think about Juan. I wonder if he is currently enjoying his retirement in gorgeous Spain. His natural leadership ability went unnoticed during his career with us. If only someone had taken the time to explain the 'why' earlier. He would have been a great manager.

Part Two

In the middle of the Continuous Improvement project, I received a call from the head office in Germany. It was Michael, my boss. My immediate reaction when I heard his voice was, "No, please don't bring me back to Germany, I am not done with Spain!" but I needn't have worried. "What do you know about [18]Empieza Por Educar?" he asked.

"They are some sort of leadership program for gifted students," I answered. I had heard about the program before. Our company had been a long-time sponsor and Michael had been an avid advocate for its purpose. He explained that I was about to put a group of thirty-five to forty of these ambitious graduate students through a crash course in change management. They would then be deployed to schools in under-resourced areas across Spain. The program had been facing a lot of resistance from the students.

The training sessions went off smoothly. It was an uplifting experience working with these smart, passionate, and motivated young adults. Several of them had already spent time volunteering in far-off places like Nepal and Africa, but because of the state of the economy in Spain, they had instead chosen to enhance their resumés with a two-year volunteering stint with Empieza Por Educar.

---

[18] Empieza por Educar was founded in 2010 to help eliminate school failure and educational inequalities in Spain. Their mission is to build a movement of change agents that - in collaboration with others - contribute in helping all children, starting with the most vulnerable, have meaningful lives through education. To achieve their mission they attract the best university graduates and select them for a professional development program.

The application process is tough. Each graduate was handpicked for the program, based on his or her exceptional performance during their studies and their can-do attitude and commitment for a better future, as idealistic it may sound at first. This was when I met the talented Estefania. She was part of this group that I would train before she headed off to central Spain. There Estefania would be working on a climate education project in a rural school. I was surprised when she called me barely a week after she had left for central Spain.

"How is the program going?" I asked.

"Terribly!" She replied.

"Oh no, what's the issue?"

"These children... They don't want me here. They have zero interest in what I have to say." Her voice sounded strained.

"You mean they're not motivated?" I wondered. "Worse than that, these kids just don't care... About anything." After I chatted with Estefania for a while, I started to develop a sense of the underlying issue. "They've lost hope," I said. "Yes. That's it exactly. To them, everything is pointless. I don't know what to do," she concluded.

Estefania's students were finding it extremely difficult to imagine any kind of future other than a lifetime of drudgery. And who could blame them? Every day they were first-hand witnesses to the hardships their families were facing. They would walk past closed-up shops and businesses on their way to school. Little wonder then that it was hard for them to grasp the value of their education when so many of their parents, aunties, and uncles, were unemployed and living on social benefits.

"I have an idea," I told her.

Over the next several days I coached the graduate teacher via email and by phone on the concept of Backward Imaging*.

I explained to Estefania that Backward Imaging is quite a clever technique, often used in managing change and I described how far removed it was from some visualisation techniques where practitioners tell people that it's enough to simply dream of a future scenario to manifest that circumstance.

[19]Backward Imaging is akin to painting a picture of a desired future, but then actually figuring out how to get there, step by step. Instead of Estefania's students trying to imagine the seemingly impossible task of getting out of their cycle of poverty through education, their current reality was the beginning point of their lives; I suggested that she should rather encourage them to start with the end in mind and work their way back.

"By doing this, you can work with them to break down those big, insurmountable goals into smaller, manageable tasks. It will help them to create a clear roadmap of the next steps to change their future," I added. When I next spoke with the young leader she was in much better spirits. "I asked them to imagine the kind of future world they wanted to be in once they graduate from university just like you said!"

Once the group painted this world, she had taken them back incrementally until the penny had dropped. They realised that to attain the house and car they desired; they needed a job that paid well. To get a job that paid well, they needed an education.

---

[19] Backward imaging takes people on a journey to the future state and works back from this in preparation for change.

Estefania used the technique to great effect with her charges when discussing climate change. Her students painted a picture of a world with adequate water, food, and no pollution. She had them map backward all the steps that would need to be taken to mitigate global warming. Slowly they built a road map of every step they needed to take to reach the future they envisaged for themselves.

The teacher noticed big improvements in her student's class averages. "Even better than that, Margit, nearly every day we chat about this, and the kids are excited. They feel hope again for a brighter future for them personally and for the world."

I loved my time in Spain. It brought home the impact what properly managed change can bring to organisations and people. An effect that transcends spreadsheet data. As for Estefania, I know she impacted quite a few young people's lives with her volunteer work. Perhaps her achievements surpassed all of ours. After all, to rekindle hope when there is none, is no small feat.

Summary of key learning points

- Recognise the tribal chiefs: Often your opinion leaders are not in the boardroom but can be found in the canteens and coffee corners. These are the people whose opinions matter to others. Winning them over can spell success for any change program.

- Look for the unexpected leaders: They might be lurking in your team and may be the people you least expect.

- Show a compelling and relatable future: To help people visualise and understand the future, inviting them to do a Backward Imaging exercise can help them discover the 'why' and the 'how' behind a course of action.

- Manage perceptions: We change practitioners, and our change champions should not see us as spies but as ears to what is holding other people b**ack.**

Strength in Numbers

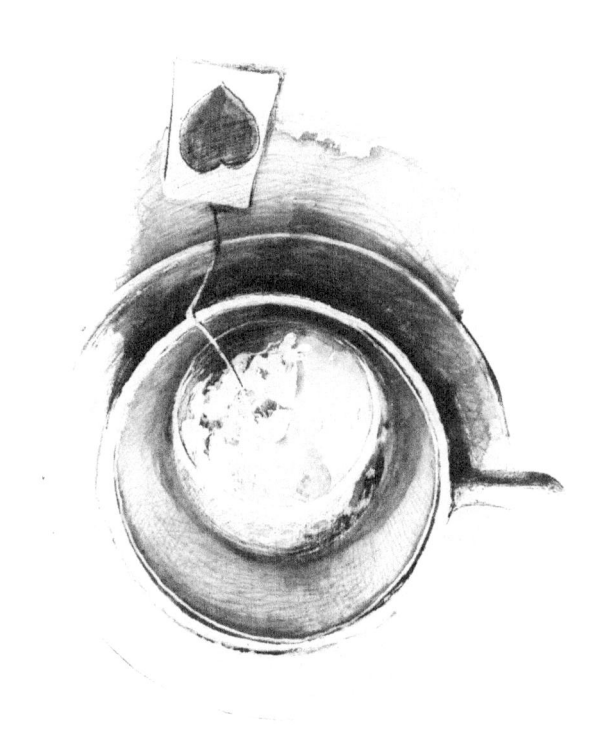

LEVERAGING COLLECTIVE WISDOM

"Coming together is a beginning, staying together is progress, and working together is success."
– Henry Ford

"No!"

The word hung in the air like a bad smell. His tone had no malice, just an unequivocal one-word rebuttal to my proposed solution. I didn't know what to do. The silence stretched on for an age, begging one of us to break it with a word, an explanation, a movement, anything. I stood in shock, looking at him with no words coming into my head.

Seldom had any of my ideas been turned down before, never like this. It is not because I am super talented and know every answer that I tend to get to 'yes' more often than not. It is because I usually don't have all the answers but I take great care to compile every bit of data I can before a project. My energy when tasked with a change project is enormous and my relentless research often means I have critical information at my fingertips. Because of this, I was more used to being congratulated by my superiors for my work ethic and strategy than being rebuffed. The hard "no," hung awkwardly between me and the group of unsmiling senior managers who had just watched me deliver my presentation.

"OK, thank you for your feedback. I will be in touch next week," I said over my shoulder as I walked out of the room.

Fresh from my successes in Asia Pacific, my change toolbox was brimful of strategies that had been stress tested by dozens of culturally complicated change projects I had worked on there.

Nothing I had experienced prepared me for this blunt response by our management in the Netherlands.

Some might call me overconfident, I guess I was, but I promise my confidence was borne out of preparation, not cockiness.

When I returned to our head office in Germany, I went over my presentation, picking apart every detail to try and understand what had gone wrong. The project was an important one. Our company had grown into a giant, and this growth had come from launching new business units and merging or acquiring others.

This led to an overlapping of systems and processes. Specifically affected were HR, IT and Finance. Four divisions operated in the Benelux region and most of my stakeholders were based in the Netherlands.

Each of the divisions operated different HR processes. Complicating things was that all four of the division's HR processes weren't just vastly different; they were also inefficient legacy systems that required site visits sometimes from HR personnel. The staff loved these visits and often dragged out their leave and pension discussions over a leisurely coffee.

The proposed amalgamation of the four HR departments would bring operational efficiency, benefiting our employees.

Improving the HR experience had also yielded surprising benefits elsewhere in our group. Customer satisfaction spiked almost immediately after implementation in those areas, and operating profits increased. How could this be? The answer is quite simple when one studies the data. The improved HR services for staff meant that employees are happier, a happy team is easier to retain and their productivity increases. This, in turn, results in enhanced customer satisfaction and retention. Delighted customers spend more.

Our new HR solution would also bring all 6,000 employees affected into a single streamlined system. The pleasant but laborious onsite coffee visits by the friendly HR team would be replaced by a unified online solution that would empower staff to execute their HR requests in minutes instead of weeks. It was shifting the mindset of 6,000 employees from in-person HR to online, once the Netherlands pilot implementation had run its course, that I expected would be the most challenging. I was wrong.

The project was important. For the first time, staff would share an equivalent work experience with no division favoured over another. There would be more automation and quicker turnaround for many requests, too. I sat at my desk mulling over the *program's Why, What and How* for what seemed like the hundredth time.

Why? - Streamlined efficiencies save money and give every employee an identical positive HR experience. We would have happier customers transacting, more business and profits would increase.

What? - We would set up Shared HR Service Centres providing employees with efficient and standardised services and tools.

How? - By creating an easy HR platform for our staff to understand and access.

I was not the one who came up with those statements, but it was my role to facilitate the right discussion with the key stakeholders and to get them all on the same page. The new unified HR solution's pilot was to be implemented in the critical Netherlands market first. I was still sitting there when Jan rapped on my open door. Jan was a tall, athletic Dutchman with copper hair and perpetually red cheeks. He would be responsible for implementing the new system and service centre when it was launched.

"How did it go?" He asked.

"They said no."

Jan had asked me to meet with the management team after he had failed several times to make any progress on the change front. He quickly brought them on board with his brilliant technical planning and project milestones. The problem was with the people plan. There were ongoing concerns from the leaders and none of our approaches resonated with them.

It irked me to admit to Jan that I had not managed to move the project forward with our plan to bring our employees on board.

"I told you this would be a challenge," Jan smiled at me. "They want to move forward; they're just not convinced we know how to tackle the expected staff resistance as well as they do."

"I know," I replied. "But I think I may have a plan."

"What are you thinking about?" he said.

"Have you ever heard of Peter Senge?" I asked.

"No, I don't think I have."

I am unsure if it was when I was with AIESEC or at university when I first came across Peter Senge's work. He is the founder of the Society of Organisational Learning. He is also the author of a quote that impacted me so much that I wrote it on the inside cover of my favourite notebook. *"People don't resist change. They resist being changed!"* "Jan let's go and see them again next week. See if you can get us into their diaries," I continued.

At the next meeting, I tried a completely different strategy. Instead of arriving with a presentation deck outlining the steps they must take to avoid employee resistance, I arrived empty-handed.

"Would you mind taking me through the rationale behind the project one more time?" I asked innocently. The meeting room whiteboards started to fill with writing; the managers taking turns to show their expertise. Whenever there was a pause, I would ask another open-ended question. Soon a chaotic picture emerged as the top leaders enthusiastically wrote up every pain point. It was clear that for our employees, the current staff experience was something of a lottery. HR outcomes would differ vastly for identical requests across the four divisions. It wasn't just unfair. It was expensive.

The pressing need for the project's technical implementation was scrawled across every whiteboard in the room. Just then, I learnt what the roadblock was.

"We have our implementation plans!" the manager exclaimed. "These are our people. We know them. I don't see how you head office people will be able to manage resistance better than we can."

And there it was. "You may be right. May I see where you are in the process?" I asked. It became evident that their planning had not progressed very far at all.

"You know, I bet I could enrich your plan a bit. Just by adding some benchmarks and good practices." They started to listen. "We know that the change is necessary, of course," I stated, pointing at the whiteboards. "But where do you think everyone is on the denial/ resistance/exploration/acceptance curve?" I was referring to the Kübler-Ross grief cycle which has similarities to the emotions experienced by employees when teams are faced with significant changes. In reality, we all experience these emotional phases every time we encounter substantial change, whether at work or at home.

My aha! moment came after each senior manager confidently stated they were in either phase three or four, meaning, they were ready to explore the new reality and accept what is to come.

"How can you be in phase three or four when you have not even developed a final plan?" I asked quietly. Over the coming weeks, I looked for opportunities to incorporate parts of the plans they had considered implementing. I would use their terminology and even modify some of my own so that the original plans, Jan and I had created, looked almost identical to the ones developed in the Netherlands.

Jan attempted to high-five me as we left the final strategy acceptance meeting. His timing was off though, as at that moment, the management team, the same team that had been stonewalling us for so long, exited the meeting room and caught us with our hands awkwardly in mid-air.

The mistake I made during my early interactions with management was a failure to give sufficient weight to the perspectives and concerns of the local stakeholders. I am lucky to have spent so much time navigating complex cross-cultural negotiations in the East. This experience evaporated when I first encountered the straight-talking Dutch. In Asia, I learnt to avoid causing offence during exchanges. Often, this would mean approaching a topic obliquely instead of head-on. Communication there is an art form. It is something I loved learning and why my immersion in other cultures has been so beneficial to my business. The Dutch often have a direct and to-the-point way of communicating that can be wrongly perceived. I wish I had read [20]Erin Meyer's work on her Culture Map at that point in my career. It would have helped me arrive at this understanding without having to figure it all out for myself.

Understanding that our perceived interpretation of exchanges may be the mark is crucial for change leaders and practitioners to learn.

Was I being duplicitous by selectively incorporating their ideas into my own and making the proposed solution feel like a locally developed initiative? When negotiating change, acceptance and progress are key objectives. A skilled change practitioner should be open-minded enough to remain adaptable without losing sight of the ultimate aim. Cooperative creation is key to smoothing over egos and vested interests. Embracing these diverse viewpoints and digging into my change toolbox to leverage existing frameworks are a thrilling part of my work.

---

[20] The Culture Map provides a framework for handling intercultural differences in business and illustrates how different cultures perceive the world.

Often, we don't have to reinvent the wheel to achieve success. There are plenty of amazing benchmarks and best practices out there to learn from; just as there is exceptional talent right there on the shop floor. This story would not be complete if I didn't tell you about the outcome of the project. Before I do, let me introduce Jo. Jo is a little dynamo of a man with some of the highest emotional intelligence I have ever encountered. I would love to claim that it was all due to Jan and myself and our 'brilliant' plan that saw the new system eagerly adopted by our 6,000 employees. We measured this by the number of 'tickets' or actionable requests on the system. The engagement was near 50 per cent within months of implementation. Here I have to give credit to our colleague Jo. He would lead meetings among our change team before and during the rollout. With charm and skill, he would counter objections and answer queries. As a project manager, with help from our global program team's experts, we worked together to get our change champions on the same page about the *What, When* and *How*. With tireless patience, he led the final step of the operation.

There is a wonderful quote by Antoine de Saint-Exupéry: *"If you want to build a ship, don't drum up people to collect wood and don't assign them tasks and work, but rather teach them to long for the endless immensity of the sea."*

I believe this was Jan's and Jo's strategy. They drummed up excitement about instant HR answers that had our people excited to use the platform.

As soon as we stopped pushing our agenda, as well thought-out and technically correct as it was, and we started actively involving our straight-talking stakeholders, the negotiations changed.

When aligning new initiatives with existing strategies, we can navigate complex challenges and lead our organisations toward a positive outcome.

My last bit of advice? Remember to save the high-fives for when you have safely left the building!

Summary of key learning points

- Understand and address stakeholders' perspectives and concerns. Co-create the plan with key leaders and the local change team.

- Leverage existing frameworks and best practices for successful change. No need to keep reinventing the wheel. What you need is right there in your change management toolbox.

- Adapt communication styles to different cultural contexts. What you hear may not be what is meant.

- Actively involve stakeholders in the change process for greater ownership and enthusiasm. Teach your team to long for the endless immensity of the sea.

From Jungle to Safe Harbour

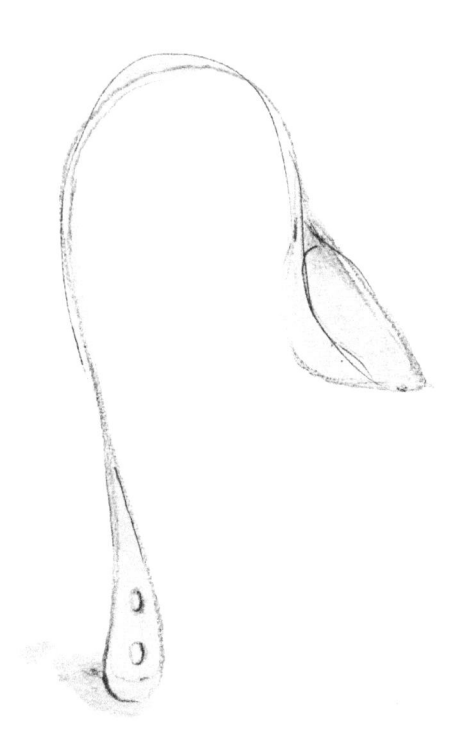

LEADING TRANSFORMATION IN THE CORPORATE JUNGLE

A ship is safe in harbour, but that is not what ships are for."
- John A. Shedd

the only constant is change, can there ever be a safe harbour? And if the safest harbour is transient, is there ever an end to any journey? There is a group of change mavericks attracting attention in the workplace. A resilient group of women and men, outliers, who have chosen to equip themselves with the skills needed to embrace change. These mavericks have cast off the security of *the way it was* in favour of the *way it must be*. And smart corporate leaders are paying attention. While great leaders know what to do, great change leaders know what to do *next*.

For clarity, perhaps the preceding sentences should read: "While great leaders know what to do. Great change leaders know what to do next *to bring teams along on the journey*." There is nothing more useless than a brilliant strategic idea left unexecuted. I love the quote at the start of this section. It is by author and theologian John A. Shedd, *"A ship is safe in harbour, but that is not what ships are for"*.

Change leaders are the equivalent of Shedd's safe harbour. It is the change mavericks who push against prevailing tides and guide the corporations on their watch safely into uncharted waters. We are the safe harbour. Today is an important day for me. Three years ago, I was seated a few tables away, about to meet my Belgian client Max. I am again inside *that lovely café*, and I have just sat down to finish writing the last chapter of my book. The chapter you're reading now. The bicycle hanging on the wall at the entrance is still in its place. The colourful walls behind me are unchanged too. I catch the eye of the server behind the bar, who will no doubt come over in a minute to take my tea order. I have my trusty *remarkable* tablet with my notes, and I am typing these words on my laptop. Reliving my experiences through notes and photographs has released many memories of my incredible journey. Not a single day passes without me being grateful for the opportunities I have enjoyed over the years. I am exceptionally lucky. Each chapter recounted an event that brought me a learning experience.

On the face of it, this book should have been easy to write. All I had to do was tell my stories and share which change principle I learnt from them. But now, common writer's wisdom dictates that I leave you with a nugget of knowledge to remember. Something so important and valuable that, in its own right, is sufficient reward for the time you have spent reading this book. But alas, there is no hack; no one-sized solution to every change problem, no magic wand. I will instead leave you with food for thought. I could use that cup of tea at this point.

Some experts argue that the change management movement was set into motion when [21]Kurt Lewin published his first book, 'A Dynamic Theory of Personality: Selected Papers' back in 1935. That book is made up of a collection of his early papers and laid the foundation for Lewin's* work on group dynamics and organisational change.

I believe that our industry is older than that, much older. Could Heraclitus be the father of the change management movement? I want to think he was. If you're unfamiliar with the famous philosopher's work, I am sure you will be with his quotes. He is the author of gems like, *"No man ever steps in the same river twice, for it's not the same river and he's not the same man."*

---

[21] Kurt Lewin stated that groups are dynamic and powerful beings which have power to influence individuals and communities.

If you're still uncertain who [22]Heraclitus is, you will almost certainly have read these words on a PowerPoint slide, "*The only constant in life is change.*" Heraclitus lived in 500 BCE and was the first philosopher to share his thoughts on reality and the universe. He believed that change is fundamental, and everything is constantly in flux.

How is it possible that we have been talking about the certainty of change for more than 2,523 years, give or take a decade, and yet so many of our leaders continue to struggle with change? Meanwhile, the most intelligent people on the planet have driven us forward technologically with AI, self-driving cars and solutions to climate catastrophe. A colleague asked me to choose one takeaway from this book I want my readers to remember. Without hesitating, I told her I wanted readers to realise that *Change Matters*. Very much.

Change champions, influencers, and managers may even be the most critical people in any business. What use is it to develop world-beating strategies and systems if management can't bring their teams along on the ride?

There are companies that embrace agility and change management as core principles. Do you want to know who they are? Look no further than the handful of most valuable companies in any niche. The manufacturer of the mobile phone in your pocket is likely to be one of them. Irrefutably investing in change teams can lead to transformative growth, market dominance, and sustained success.

---

[22] **Heraclitus** was an ancient Greek pre-Socratic philosopher from the city of Ephesus, which was then part of the Persian Empire

The ability to adapt rapidly enables firms to seize new opportunities before their competitors. Throughout this book, I have spoken of the importance of identifying and bringing change champions on board. Too often, these key individuals' contributions are only recognised after a critical change event has occurred. It is impossible to 'adapt rapidly and seize opportunities' when a change team hasn't been mobilised or trained yet.

Is it a crazy idea for organisations to invest in dedicated change teams as much as they do in product development? In my experience, firms that ensure they have dedicated resources trained and ready to drive innovation, explore new opportunities, and fuel long-term growth also have no problem retaining the best talent.

I have written and rewritten this section several times, and there is still no sign of the server. Slowly the realisation is growing on me that this is not the *café* I remember.

The music is obtrusive, and the colourful mural behind me, a little less colourful.

"Oh goodness! Is that a teabag string draped over the cup's lip on the uncleared table next to me?" It is time to go.

Summer is around the corner. This year, instead of visiting my parents in Békés, Hungary they are coming to see us here in Geneva. Of course, they will spend time with our girls, but I know that after putting their granddaughters to bed, the grandparents will sit with me for hours listening attentively while I tell them all about my adventures.

It is a family tradition that my mom makes her 'floating islands' dessert whenever they visit. Somehow the flavours have remained perfectly consistent over the years; every delicious mouthful transporting me back to my beautiful Békés. My husband will also be listening attentively to the conversation encouraging me to take on the next challenge. A long time ago my dad made me promise not to become a teacher. I will ask him this summer if he realises that this is exactly what I have become. I teach change management, and I am proud that I have such important work to do. We all have important work to do.

You know that incredible progress has been made when the people you least expect, stand up to make a difference. I have referenced people of unassailable character who have stood up from their workbenches and delivery trucks, who have used their coffee corner influence and their lunch breaks to bring about change. The real change champions are hardly ever found where you expect them to be. They are stepping up and making things better right where they are.

An oasis needn't be an elusive mirage in the desert or the wilderness. With an agile change team ready to adapt quickly to every advantage, a refreshing oasis could be a metaphor for the culture running deeply throughout your company.

At the rear of this book, you will find a page of resources to explore. I have included my mom's 'floating islands' recipe and a link to my website where I am building a library of change content to help my fellow change mavericks on our journey.

We are all in this together because **Change Matters.**

Acknowledgements

I want to take a moment to express my deepest gratitude to the extraordinary individuals who accompanied me on this incredible journey of creating Change Matters. The seed of this idea sprouted in my mind back in 2019, and now, thanks to your unwavering support, you can hold the tangible result in your hands. Writing this book was a rollercoaster ride, but the presence of these amazing individuals filled me with energy, engagement, and sometimes just a comforting hug, keeping me motivated through every challenge we encountered along the way—and believe me, there were plenty!

As an author, I have experienced tremendous personal growth throughout this process, and I want to extend my heartfelt thanks to each and every one of you for being an integral part of this transformative journey.

To my loving husband, José Luis, I am eternally grateful for your steadfast support, countless cups of tea, and encouraging words throughout the ups and downs of this creative endeavor. You always reminded me of the bigger picture of life, and how this book will stand as a cherished milestone for our family.

To my daughters, Evelyn and Ariana, your understanding and unwavering support have been my rock throughout the writing process. You have continuously reminded me that life is more than just a book; it is about us, our family. My hope is that as you grow up, you will see me not only as your loving mom but also as a woman who believes in and stands up for human-centered change.

To my parents, Ernő and Margit, thank you for instilling in me lasting values centered around people, growth, and lifelong learning in every endeavor I pursue.

To Andrew Mark, my exceptional author, coach and collaborative writer for his support and partnership through these three years of writing *Change Matters*. He has helped me find my voice in more ways I can describe. He delved into the depth of my ideas, refined them and weaved them into a compelling narrative.

To Dali de Clair, my dedicated and meticulous proofreader, thank you for your unwavering commitment to excellence and attention to detail. Your insights not only stimulated my mind but also touched my heart and spirit, elevating the overall reader experience.

To German Valencia, my mentor, your wisdom, encouragement, and expertise have guided me along this path. You have been my guide, cheerleader, and mirror, enabling me to view my drafts from the perspective of business leaders and inspiring me to reach new heights as a business owner.

To Lisa Ferland, my trusted crowdfunding for authors consultant, your invaluable expertise and support were instrumental in bringing this book to fruition. You have taught me so much about audience building, engagement, and value proposition, and connected me with numerous inspiring authors along the way.

To Matías Thourte, my incredibly talented illustrator, your artistic genius has taken my book to another level. Your illustrations have added a captivating and visually engaging dimension to Change Matters.

To Sole Bassett my graphic designer and dear friend, and Maryna Beukes, my talented book cover artist, thank you for sparking my imagination when it comes to creating a visual experience for the readers. Your dedication and willingness to go the extra mile are deeply appreciated.

To Amod Date, Serene Wong, Michel Beutler, Michael Hagemann, and Verena Amonat, thank you for being amazing change leaders who have inspired me on my professional journey, both within the corporate world and beyond.

To my VIP launch team and core supporters of the Kickstarter crowdfunding campaign, your help in spreading the word about the purpose behind Change Matters and in self-publishing this book with the necessary resources has been invaluable. Months before it went to print, together we managed to secure 642 pre-orders from thirty-seven countries!

My deepest gratitude goes out to:

Adelheid Moxon, Aditi Rasquinha, Aibek Dunaev, 'Ain Aid, Akos Jakobsen, Alfred Bruce-Micah, Amit Singh, Ana Hristova, Andrea Kondacs, Andreas Baller, Andreea Murlis, Andreia Leonard, Anna Olsson, Anne Hofmann, Anne Olsson, Anna Szoke, Anna Hofmann, Anne van Huijstee, Antonia Adeyemi, April Anne Sese, Arthur Seidl, Astrid Mochtarram, Balázs Kertész, Bart van Grinsven, Ben Kubik, Ben Lechner, Berry Crook, Boyan Yordanov, Brenda Chapel, Brian Boyd, Brian Hayes, Britta Mues-Walter, Camille Jayne Ang, Carl Hodges, Carmen Mitroescu, Carolina Yeo, Caroline Dowling, Caroline Mellows, Chieko Tamakawa, Chitra Shine, Chris Byrne, Christian Holyoak, Chuck Kalnbach, Ciara Kissane, Claudia Paulsen, Clement Cohen, Dominique Turner, Colm Tarpey, Csilla Gamos, Cyriel Kortleven, Cyrilla Costello, D Scott Ross, Dali De Clercq, Dan Gabor Horvath, Daniel Ahlers, Daniela Citu, Daniela Moaes, David Cornick, David Hausmann, Deema Ghata-Aura, Deepak Bansal, Deirdre Carey, Devrim Leonard, Dew Neo, Diana Herrera, Dra Adela Viveros Añorve, Donald Angle, Dora Bodo, Eka Sriyuni, Elizabeth O'Brien, Ellen Brian, Elvin Wong, Emma Vallin, Enrica Fantini, Eszter Koncz, Eva Mattheeussen, Eva Stanbury, Eva Szczurek, Ewa Bronowicz, Fabio Grassi, Faisol Ahmed, Fiona Burnett, Fiona Gould, Florian Schwartz, Gabor Zsikla, Geraldine Oades-Sese, German Valencia, Ginel Postolea, Giulia Merati, Grace Ma, Graeme Noon, Graham Bastable, Greg Jones, Gyula Farkas, Hari Prasad Nair, Helen von Dadelszen, Ian Sanderson, Ignacio Lucini, Igor Zygaldo, Ilona Pesti, Irina Albanese, Iulia Serban, Jacqui Woodall, James Banningan, Janice Ng Yen Li, Jeff Caselden, Jennifer Topinka, Jiska Janssen, Jon Ferland, Jona Interino, Joost Koolen, José Hop, José Paul Mathew, Judit Schneider, Dr Judy Lundy, Jules Saad, Julian Wong, Julie de Meyer, Julie Dwyer, Justin Lim, Kai Chan, Katica Ivan, Katie Wrighton, Klikke Sietel, Kriszta Major-Fábián, Krisztina Bana, Laetitia Johnson, Lana

Mamone, Lars Voedisch, Laszlo Rab, Laszlo Takacs, Lionel Alexander, Lisa Niermann, Lucian Muresan, Luis René Ramirez Padilla, Luis Villalobos, Lynn Bruines, Maja Radakovic, Malin Sandbacka, Mandy Bronsil, Maria Grotle, Mária Hidvégi, Maria Savranska, Maria Stefansdottir, Marion Rupp, Marthe Kortenbruck, Mary Fortuna Vaz, Maryna Jarzabek Ragunathan, Matthew Neagle, Mayuko Endo, Melissa Tiro Park, Merima Baralić de Ramírez, Michael Mole, Michael Sullivan, Michal Kostic, Michel Beutler, Midia Fiuza, Monika Baran, Natalia Pliszczak, Niamh dee, Nicole Bohl, Nina Noonan, Nina Wohlleben, Nisarg Meha, Nora Tollenaar-Szanto, Norma Murphy, Ozana Corkery, Pal Bjelkengren, Patrick Siffert, Patrick Wall, Paul Lyons, Paul Ryan, Pauliina Rasi, Perasa Philipp, Petra Lehmann, Petra Michel, Phil Murphy, Phililppa Yeo-Dundas, Pooja Monga, Rachel Moosa, Rachelle Woodsford, Rebecca Sladdin, Rhiannon Cooke, Rita Pátkai-Major, Rob Byrne, Robert Aiello, Robert Bartram, Robert Mustart, Roberto Cruz, Roberto Villamil Alvarez, Robin Goel, Rohit Ramesh TR Rohit Sathe, Ruchira Neotia, Sabrina Van Bellinghen, Sandor Laczko, Sanita Auseja, Sarah Vader, Sean Gayer, Sharmee Mannar, Shweta Gupta, Sidhart Rupani, Sietske Claessens, Simone Anzboeck, Sole Bassett, Sonam Jain, Srini Raghunathan, Stephen Lynch, Stephen Smith, Steve Migunda, Steven De Wit, Steven Light, Sven Gade, Syed Anis ur Rahman, Szilvia Vitos, Tamara Rittershaus, Tania Moloney, Tara Ryan, Teresa Lee, Terézia Nagy, Thomas Hayes, Thorsten Jowanowitsch, Tibor Farkas, Tibor Kadar, Tibor Torok, Tímea Nagy, Tugba Sert, Ujju Sagar, Ulrika Karlsoon, Vega Chang, Verena Amonat, Vicky Oikonomou, Viktoria Vero, Virginia Jimenez, Vivek Subbaiah, Wing Huo, Yoshito Darmon-Shimamori, Zsofi Tonelli, Zuzana Rintelova.

To every one of the 149 Beta Readers who took the time to read the sample chapter of my book and provided invaluable insights, feedback, and recommendations to fine-tune its structure and style, I am incredibly grateful for your contribution.

To Kat Decena, my dedicated Virtual Assistant, thank you for diligently overseeing every detail and effectively liaising with everyone in my community, ensuring that communications flowed smoothly even during the busiest of days.

To all my clients who have entrusted me to practice what I preach, working on and consulting change programs, large and small—I extend my heartfelt thanks. It is through your collaboration that I have been able to share countless stories and insights. A special mention goes to Adidas, Aer Lingus, Amazon, Arms Trade Treaty Secretariat, Boston Scientific, Deutsche Post DHL, Dublin City Council, Edith Cowan University, Ericsson, ERIKS, Glanbia, Irish Management Institute, Hotel School The Hague, Laya Healthcare, Medicine for Malaria Venture, Nestle, Ornua, Pfiyer, Qualtrics, Sanmina, SK Biotek, University of Oregon, Workday, and many others.

Finally, as I bring this acknowledgement section to a close, I want to express my profound appreciation, knowing that no words can fully convey the depth of my gratitude. To all those who have believed in me, cheered me on, and extended a helping hand along this journey, I thank you from the bottom of my heart. This book would not have been possible without your presence in my life, and I am eternally grateful for your unwavering support.

"Madártej"
My mom's famous *Floating Islands* recipe

Ingredients:
4 large eggs
100 grams (1/2 cup) granulated sugar
480 ml (2 cups) milk
1 teaspoon vanilla extract
Pinch of salt
Caramel sauce or other desired toppings (e.g., toasted almonds, fresh berries)

Method:
1. Separate the egg whites from the yolks and place them in separate bowls.
2. In the bowl with the egg yolks, whisk in 100 grams (1/4 cup) of granulated sugar until the mixture becomes pale and creamy.
3. In a saucepan, heat the milk with the vanilla extract until it reaches a simmer.
4. Gradually pour the hot milk into the egg yolk mixture while whisking continuously.
5. Return the mixture to the saucepan and cook over low heat, stirring constantly, until it thickens to a custard consistency. This should take about 10-15 minutes.
6. Remove the custard from heat and let it cool. Place a layer of plastic wrap directly on the surface of the custard to prevent a skin from forming.
7. In the bowl with the egg whites, whisk them until soft peaks form. Gradually add the remaining 50 grams (1/4 cup) of granulated sugar while continuing to whisk until the meringue becomes glossy and holds stiff peaks.

Continued overleaf

8. Fill a large saucepan halfway with water and bring it to a simmer.

9. Using two spoons, shape the meringue mixture into oval-shaped quenelles (egg-like shapes) and gently place them into the simmering water. Poach them for about 2 minutes on each side, until they are firm and cooked through.

Remove them from the water with a slotted spoon and let them drain on a paper towel.

10. To serve, pour some custard into serving bowls or dishes. Place one or two poached meringues on top of the custard.

11. Garnish with caramel sauce or any other desired toppings like toasted almonds or fresh berries.

Serve my mom's Floating Island dessert chilled or at room temperature when you next celebrate a family adventure. Magic might happen!

Are you stuck with a change conundrum? Reach out through my website where I have a growing library of change-related resources, or leave a question on my LinkedIn page. *Because Change Matters!*

www.margittakacs.com